Scottish
Witches

To Nan, Fiona and Lesley . . . May they always enjoy the sheer enchantment of life and may all their special dreams come true!

Scottish Witches

By Charles W. Cameron

Jarrold Publishing, Norwich

About the author

Charles W. Cameron has had an interest in the supernatural for many years. He lectures on the paranormal, witchcraft and demonology, and the occult, and has made numerous television appearances. He also prepares daily astrological horoscopes for local radio and has written and narrated radio programmes such as 'Beyond the Unknown' and 'Friday Frightener'. Editor and publisher of *The Cauldron*, a magazine devoted to strange and unusual magic, he has had many books published on various aspects of the supernatural and has written numerous articles and short stories on the subject. He is married, with two daughters, and lives in Haddington, East Lothian.

Acknowledgements

My grateful thanks, as always, to my wife, family and friends for their sincere patience and understanding during the research and actual writing of this book.

In addition, my very sincere thanks to my publishers for their infinite patience while waiting for the completed manuscript.

Charles W. Cameron

Front cover illustration: Don Fisher

ISBN 0-7117-0451-1
© Jarrold Publishing 1984, 1990
Published by Jarrold Publishing, Norwich
First published 1984
Second edition 1990
Printed in Great Britain. 2/90

Contents

Introduction

Witchcraft flourished in Scotland, particularly between the sixteenth and seventeenth centuries, and tales of witches, warlocks,
magic and ghosts are closely interwoven into the fabric of Scottish
history. The story of those who followed the Old Religion is fascinating as it describes their strange powers and sometimes terrifying
supernatural experiences. It is also deeply tragic. Relentlessly
persecuted, witches were tortured and executed with a violence
and cruelty unimaginable today.

Witchcraft has a long history in Scotland. It can be traced as far
back as the fourth century AD and it is said that when St Patrick
fled to Ireland he was chased out of the country by witches incensed
by his devotion and piety; furious at not being able to pursue him
over running water (St Patrick sailed to Ireland from the Clyde),
they hurled rocks after him. The fortress of Dumbartonshire is said
to be one of the masses of rock thrown by the infuriated witches. At
the end of the seventh century, King Kenneth was so alarmed at
the rapid spread of sorcery in Scotland that he issued a special
decree condemning all jugglers, wizards, witches, conjurors and
necromancers to death. Few people, however, took this decree
seriously and the practice of witchcraft continued to flourish.

The first recorded case of witch-burning seems to have taken
place in Forres in the tenth century, after King Duffus, the
seventy-eighth King of Scotland, fell ill of a strange and
mysterious sickness. As the days passed the King began to pine
and wither away and the court physicians admitted that they were
completely baffled. It was rumoured that the King's illness could
only be due to one cause – witchcraft!

Some days later, news reached the court that a number of
notorious witches in Forres were believed to have met on numerous occasions for the purpose of 'taking away the life of the King'.
The Governor of Forres Castle had arrested a young girl who had
been heard to threaten the King and after 'suitable persuasion' the
girl had confessed that her mother, a notorious sorceress, and a
complete coven of Devil-worshippers were casting spells and incantations to kill the King by means of enchantment. Armed with
this information the Governor sent soldiers to the girl's house and
arrested a number of old women who were caught in the act of
roasting the King's image, made in wax and suspended over a slow

fire by means of a long spit. The waxen image was smashed and trampled into dust, the witches were imprisoned and eventually burnt at the stake and King Duffus duly recovered his strength and health. On the west road of Forres there still stands an iron-clamped stone marking the spot where the witches were burned, known as 'The Witches' Stone'.

By the sixteenth century, however, a full-scale persecution of witches was under way, with an almost hysterical mania for hunting down and executing anyone found guilty of 'trafficking with His Infernal Majesty the Devil and practising diabolic arts'. Witchcraft was a criminal offence in Scotland from 1563, when it was included in statute law, until 1736, when it was repealed. (After 1736 it was possible only to prosecute for 'pretended witchcraft and to impose a maximum penalty of a year's imprisonment'.) Authorities differ very widely in their estimates of the number of witches executed in Scotland. This is not really surprising when one remembers that, especially during the seventeenth century, cases of witchcraft were so common that many of them hardly even merited a casual reference in court records. Between 1479 and 1722 it does appear, however, that over 17,000 people, mostly women, were tortured and then put to death.

As the entire estate of anyone convicted of witchcraft became the sole property of the Crown it is, perhaps, hardly surprising that witch-hunting was considered such a popular pastime. Even the cost of the trial and the material used in the execution fire were deducted from the victim's estate before it passed to the Crown, and the wealthier the victim the more certain the final verdict.

In this book you will discover strange legends of Scottish witches, legends of Devil worship and curious tales of weird happenings. You will also read the history of man's inhumanity to man, the tragic story of human beings who were persecuted because of the ignorance, stupidity and blind superstition of their fellow men whose own fear and greed blackened and scorched the noble pages of Scottish history.

Charles W. Cameron

News from Scotland:

DECLARING THE

DAMNABLE LIFE OF DOCTOR FIAN,

A

NOTABLE SORCERER,

WHO WAS

Burned at Edenbrough in Januarie last, 1591.

WHICH DOCTOR WAS REGISTER TO THE DEVILL THAT
SUNDRIE TIMES PREACHED AT NORTH BARRICKE
KIRKE TO A NUMBER OF NOTORIOUS WITCHES.

WITH THE

TRUE EXAMINATIONS OF THE SAID DOCTOR AND WITCHES, AS THEY UTTERED THEM IN THE PRESENCE OF THE SCOTTISH KING.

DISCOVERING

HOW THEY PRETENDED TO BEWITCH AND DROWNE
HIS MAJESTIE IN THE SEA COMMING FROM DEN-
MARKE; WITH SUCH OTHER WONDERFULL
MATTERS AS THE LIKE HATH NOT BEIN
HEARD AT ANIE TIME.

Published according to the Scottish Copie.

PRINTED FOR WILLIAM WRIGHT.

EDINBURGH:

RE-PRINTED FOR D. WEBSTER, 35, WEST COLLEGE STREET.

1820.

1 Famous witches

The North Berwick witches

One of the best-known and certainly one of the most notorious tales in the history of Scottish witchcraft is the strange story of the celebrated Dr John Fian and the infamous North Berwick witches. King James VI and I himself took a keen personal interest in this somewhat macabre affair and, in fact, presided over the official inquiry. Nearly 100 people, including the Earl of Bothwell, were arrested on charges that ranged from witchcraft to high treason. It all began because a simple servant girl was in the habit of wandering about late at night.

Geillis or Gilly Duncan was a serving-maid in the household of David Seaton, deputy bailiff of Tranent, a small town in East Lothian. Rumours reached the ears of her employer whispering of strange healing powers, miraculous cures and witchcraft, and when Seaton discovered that night after night Gilly Duncan was absent from her room he decided to take the law into his own hands. Convinced that she must be in league with the Devil and that her powers could only be due to witchcraft, Seaton tortured her then examined her for the traditional Devil's mark. When a small mark was eventually found on her throat, Seaton was firmly convinced that she was indeed in league with Satan and promptly turned her over to the appropriate authorities.

After suffering further cruel and inhumane tortures the unfortunate girl confessed and, as was usual in such cases, immediately implicated many others. Over a period of days Gilly Duncan, almost out of her mind with fear and pain, accused Agnes Sampson of Haddington, Robert Grierson, a ship's captain, and Dr John Fian, a schoolteacher at Saltpans who was also known as John Cunningham and who was said to be Bothwell's secretary. The list was endless and included a number of very wealthy and influential people. King James ordered that Agnes Sampson be brought to Holyrood Palace, where she was immediately questioned then tortured. At first she strenuously denied all the charges brought against her and despite lack of sleep and barbaric torture she maintained a grave and dignified manner. Eventually, however, she broke down and confessed that, along with many others, she had taken part in a Witches' Sabbat at North Berwick on All Hallows' Eve on 31 October 1590.

Agnes Sampson told the assembled court that the Sabbat had been held in the old haunted kirk and that its main purpose had been to destroy King James by means of devilish sorcery. According to Agnes Sampson, who herself had taken a leading part in the proceedings, over 200 witches – men and women – had sailed to North Berwick in sieves, drinking wine and singing to the accompaniment of strange musical instruments. When the unholy company reached North Berwick, Gilly Duncan met them and led them in a weird procession through the graveyard, playing a curious tune on a Jew's harp. Flickering flames from numerous black candles lit up the otherwise dark interior of the old North Berwick church and weird shadows twisted and writhed across the stone walls. The ghastly procession danced down the aisle watched by the Devil himself, who stood in the pulpit.

Questioned further by the court, Agnes Sampson declared that the Devil was dressed all in black, his face was terrible to look upon, his eyes burned with a weird unholy fire and his feet and hands were hooked claws. A number of authorities are of the opinion that it was actually the Earl of Bothwell himself who stood in the pulpit disguised as the Devil and who discussed different ways of killing King James.

Agnes Sampson then confessed that after the Sabbat she had hung up a black toad then after three days had collected its venom in an oyster-shell. A certain John Kers, one of the King's personal attendants, had been asked to provide a piece of the King's clothing and this together with the venom would have been used to cast a spell of enchantment upon the King. John Kers had refused to help, so a wax doll was made instead and a death spell was cast. Agnes Sampson admitted that this substitute spell had been unsuccessful but in order to prove that she did possess strange magical powers she whispered to the King the very words he had spoken to his young bride on their wedding-night. The horrified King admitted that she was correct, then promptly sentenced her to death.

Dr Fian was arrested but escaped from prison and fled to Saltpans only to be recaptured and brought back to Edinburgh. Fian confessed to having practised witchcraft and sorcery but only after he had been subjected to being tortured in a most barbaric fashion. His nails were torn from his fingertips then long sharp needles were thrust into the quicks of his fingers. Both legs were

North Berwick witches raising a storm

completely-crushed in the dreaded 'boot' then finally when he had confessed he was sentenced to be strangled and burned on the Castle Hill. The sentence was carried out one Saturday in January, 1591.

The Earl of Bothwell was also arrested and thrown into prison in Edinburgh Castle but he escaped and fled to the Continent.

One of the accused, Dame Euphemia Maclean, was brought to trial and a number of lawyers risked the wrath of the King by defending her. An extremely wealthy woman, Dame Maclean refused to admit to being a witch and denied all knowledge of the Sabbat at North Berwick. After an all-night sitting the jury refused to bring in a verdict and eventually the foreman was dismissed by the King, who himself directed that a verdict of guilty be given. Dame Euphemia Maclean was burned alive on 25 July 1591.

Barbara Napier, sister-in-law to the Laird of Carschoggil, and Richard Graham, a noted sorcerer, were both accused of attempting to harm the King by melting a wax picture of him over a slow fire. In addition they were also accused of trying to sink his ship by raising a storm by means of diabolical sorcery. The jury dismissed the case but this so enraged the King that he immediately ordered the entire court to be reassembled then demanded that Barbara Napier be strangled and burned at the stake and that her property be handed over to him. The entire jury were then themselves tried for deliberately allowing a known witch to go free. Barbara Napier pleaded that as she was with child she should be shown mercy and allowed to go free and after being kept in prison for some time this was done. Richard Graham was not so lucky, however, and he was burned at the stake in February 1592.

In the days that followed, many of those who had taken part in the ill-fated North Berwick Sabbat were burned alive at the stake and a pall of heavy black smoke hung over the Castle Hill; the stench of roasted flesh sickened even the hardened executioners.

Isobel Gowdie

Fascinating though the North Berwick witch trial undoubtedly was, perhaps the most interesting one was the trial of Isobel Gowdie in the year 1662.

Isobel Gowdie came from Auldearne, 3 miles east of Nairn and about 16 miles north-east of Inverness. According to the official court records Isobel Gowdie made four complete confessions, none of which were apparently extracted under the pain of torture. Unfortunately this really means very little because the term 'torture' was defined somewhat differently when applied to witch trials. Preliminary tortures – and these could include being deprived of food and drink, kept without sleep for long periods, savage beatings, limbs crushed in a vice and being cruelly stretched on a rack – were frequently ignored by the courts. Confessions thus obtained usually had the words 'The prisoner confessed without torture' written into the official records. The 'real torture' was usually kept for the final confession in order to force the suspected witch to name his or her accomplices.

Isobel Gowdie had met the Devil himself some 15 years earlier whilst she was walking between two farms in the neighbouring vicinity. She told the court that the Devil had spoken to her in the most friendly manner and had invited her to meet him again that very night in the old parish church of Auldearne. That same night she was initiated into the dark mysterious arts of witchcraft and the Devil gave her a new name, a witch name – Janet. He marked her on the shoulder then sucked some blood from the mark which he sprinkled on her head in order to baptise her. Having done this, the Devil then placed one hand on the top of her head and the other hand on the soles of her feet, and Isobel Gowdie solemnly promised that 'all that lay between would henceforth be dedicated to his service'.

The Devil then conducted a service from the pulpit and read to the assembled congregation from a large black book. When asked by the court to describe the Devil, Isobel Gowdie stated that he was 'a mickle, black, hairy man'. The congregation was then organised into covens of 13 and Isobel Gowdie named each of the 'officers' who were placed in charge, stating that the one in charge of her own particular coven was a certain John Young.

Isobel Gowdie then described to the court the various spells, charms and incantations that she and other witches in the district were in the habit of using to achieve their evil ends. Most of the spells she mentioned were of an agricultural nature – charms to secure for themselves crops belonging to any farmer they disliked. One required that an unbaptised child be taken from its grave and added to the witches' own nail parings, together with cabbage leaves and ears of corn. These strange ingredients were then finely chopped and mixed together and buried deep in a field. According to her statement, the evil charm worked and the crops failed after the witches had taken the yield for themselves.

She then described another strange spell, one clearly associated with the magic used by the 'wee folk'. A number of toads were yoked to a plough, using dog-grass for the actual harness, and with the sharpened horn of a ram providing the blade. According to Isobel Gowdie, John Young and the Devil himself then drove the plough round a certain farmer's field. The entire coven followed close behind and all of them prayed furiously to the Devil, asking that they be given the fruits of the field and that the unfortunate farmer be left with a crop of thistles and thorns. Isobel Gowdie told the court that the spell had worked and that the Devil had been pleased with them.

Next she described how a witch could make a cow stop giving milk, or raise a storm or make the wind cease to blow. To raise a storm, she said, was simple: a witch would take a piece of dampened rag, lay it on a flat stone and then beat it with a piece of wood while chanting the following incantation three times:

> I knock this rag upon this stone,
> To raise the wind in my Master's name,
> It shall not lie, until I please again!

To calm a storm, she said, was just as simple. The cloth rag would be dried, then the witch would chant three times:

> We lay the wind in the Devil's name.
> It shall not rise until we like to raise it again!

Isobel also told the court about her connection with the fairy people, describing the 'wee folk' as short, strong, very broad little people with special magical powers. Of particular interest was her description of the legendary 'Elf-Arrows' with their poisoned tips. She told how a witch might shoot these at an enemy by flicking them from his or her thumb-nail – the slightest scratch meant instant death to the unfortunate victim.

Hardly surprising was the fact that the Reverend Harry Forbes, minister of Auldearne, was a sworn enemy of the local witches and frequently loudly denounced them and their evil trade from his pulpit. On one occasion when he was taken ill the witches made up their minds to charm him to death. In order to do this they collected a weird assortment of ingredients to use with their evil incantations. A hare's liver, the flesh, entrails and gall of a toad, nail parings, grains of barley, rags and other strange objects were placed into a bag, which was soaked for some time in water. Whilst this was being done the Devil led the coven in a curious chant:

> He is lying in his bed, he is sick and sore.
> Let him lie in that bed two months and days three more,
> He shall lie in his bed and he shall be sick and sore.
> He shall lie in his bed two months and days three more!

The entire coven then went down on their knees, stretched out their arms to the Devil and implored him to destroy the minister.

The Devil told them that one of their number had to take the bag into the minister's bedroom and swing it over his bed. A certain Bessie Hay was chosen for the curious reason that 'she was on intimate terms with the said minister'! However, when she entered the room she discovered that a number of very devout and pious people were visiting him, so she was forced to leave without achieving her evil purpose. Isobel Gowdie stated that the spell did not work and the minister recovered.

During her confession Isobel Gowdie described what took place during a coven meeting and it became clear that these meetings were also an excuse for orgies of a highly sexual nature. To the horror of the court she named a number of extremely respectable and highly placed local citizens who had attended these meetings.

According to Isobel Gowdie all the members of her coven had spirits or familiars to wait upon them. Her own particular spirit was called 'Red Reiver' and was dressed entirely in black. Margaret Wilson had a spirit she called 'Swein' who was dressed in grass green and Bessie Wilson's familiar had the incredible jaw-breaking name of 'Theife-of-Hell-Wait-upon-Herself'.

Isobel Gowdie also stated that on frequent occasions she transformed herself into a cat, a hare and even, at times, a jackdaw. When questioned by the court she said that whenever she wished to become, for example, a hare she would utter the following spell:

> I shall go into a hare;
> With sorrow, and such, and great care;
> And I shall go thus in the Devil's name,
> Until I return home again.

'Whereupon,' said Isobel, 'I instantly become a hare.' To return to human shape, said Isobel, it was only necessary for her to say:

> Hare, hare, God send thee care!
> I am in a hare's likeness just now
> But I shall be in a woman's likeness even now.

To become a crow the following spell was chanted three times:

> I shall go into a crow,
> With sorrow, and such, and a black thraw!
> And I shall go in the Devil's name,
> Until I come home again!

16

To return to human form the witch uttered the following cantrip:

Crow, crow God send thee a black thraw
I was a crow just now.
But I shall be in a woman's likeness even now.
Crow, crow God send thee a black thraw.

One cannot help thinking that it would have been extremely easy for the court to have tested just how effective these spells really were but the accused, of course, had the answer to this line of reasoning by stating that once he or she was arrested the Devil immediately withdrew all magical powers.

Isobel Gowdie told the court that when she and other women were attending Sabbats they would place a broomstick in their beds beside their husbands. Having done this they would then utter the following spell:

I lay down this broom in the Devil's name
Let it not stir from hence till I come again!

Immediately the broom would take on the witch's own appearance.

When questioned about their method of transport to the Sabbats Isobel Gowdie informed the court that witches would take a length of straw, place it between their legs and then recite three times:

Horse and hattock, horse and go,
Horse and pellatis, ho! ho!

and immediately they would fly through the air.

The court records are filled with numerous spells and incantations and extremely detailed accounts of Sabbat meetings. Either Isobel Gowdie was an extremely intelligent and highly imaginative woman or she was indeed a witch and her confessions, incredible though it may seem, were true in every respect. She was the wife of a farmer and, according to a number of sources, was a very attractive young red-haired girl; why she confessed to being a witch is an enigma, but she was hanged at the West Port of Elgin and her body burned to ashes.

Isobel Haldane of Perth
One of the most fascinating cases in the history of Scottish witchcraft is that of Isobel Haldane of Perth. On 15 May in the year 1623, Isobel Haldane was brought before the sessions accused of

The High Priest of a modern witch coven

practising the evil arts of witchcraft and sorcery. After the session had prayed earnestly to God, the accused was asked whether she possessed the power to cure human beings of illness. Isobel Haldane denied this charge but was then immediately asked whether she had ever cured a certain Andrew Duncan's child.

Looking her accusers full in the face she said, 'I went to the Turret-port and took some water from there. I then brought the water to the house of Andrew Duncan. Kneeling down I prayed in the name of the Father, Son and Holy Ghost and then I washed the sick child. Next I took the child's sark [shirt] and the water and threw both of them into the river. Unfortunately on the way I spilt some of the water and this I regret, for if anyone had stepped across the water they would have fallen ill with the child's sickness.'

The session then asked her whether she had ever met or conversed with the fairy folk. The accused woman stated that when she was but 10 years old she had been taken from her bed and carried to a certain hillside. It had mysteriously opened and she was taken inside, where she had stayed for three days, from Thursday until Sunday at noon, when she had been led back to the outside world by a grey-bearded man.

Not long after this particular episode, Isobel Haldane stated, she was in a carpenter's shop owned by a man known as James Christie. Christie and one of his customers were discussing a cradle the carpenter was making for the baby his wife was expecting. According to witnesses Haldane had told the carpenter that there was no immediate rush, for the child would not be born for another five weeks. She had then prophesied that 'The child will never lie in the cradle but be born, baptised, never suck but die and taken away.' Her strange prophesy came true, and when she was asked how she knew this would be so Haldane replied that the man with the grey beard had told her. A certain John Roch (who had been the customer in the carpenter's shop) also testified that the accused had visited Margaret Buchanan, the wife of David Rind, and had told her that she would die in a few days' time. Buchanan, a woman in perfect health, had at first ignored the warning but several days after receiving the dreadful pronouncement she wasted away and died. When the session asked her how she knew that this would happen Isobel Haldane again said that the grey-bearded man had told her.

The session then called another witness, a certain Patrick Ruthven, a skinner from Perth, who had once been bewitched by a witch known as Margaret Hornscleugh. Isobel Haldane had agreed to attempt to 'unwitch' him; she did this by telling him to lie on his bed then lying on top of him herself. After muttering a few strange words she told him that he was now normal and free from the spell. Ruthven stated that this was indeed true, and Isobel Haldane admitted the charge.

Stephen Ray from Muirton told the assembled court that some three years earlier he had found out that the accused had stolen some beer from Balhoussie Hall. Ray chased after her and demanded that she return the stolen beer. According to him, Haldane had been extremely annoyed and had clapped him on the shoulder declaring, 'Go thy way! Thou shalt not win thyself a morsel of bread for a year and a day!' Ray stated that the evil curse had come to pass and he had wasted away, heavily diseased. According to the court records, Haldane admitted stealing the beer but said that she had only said to Ray, 'He that delivered me from the fairy folk shall take amends on thee!'

Pressed to confess further, Isobel Haldane stated that she had once gone in secret to the Holy Well of Ruthven and brought back some water in order to heal John Gow's sick child. Isobel Haldane also admitted that she had once concocted a brew from star-grass leaves gathered by her son, and had used it to cure many sick children by letting them drink it.

It was common for country folk to consult the local village 'wise woman' when one of the family was ill, particularly in the case of children, even though this was considered to be just as dangerous as actually being a witch, and the penalties were just as severe. One story about Isobel Haldane tells how her advice was sought by the wife of David Morrice of Perth, who was convinced that her child was a changeling. Haldane came to see the child and declared that it was indeed a fairy changeling. She prescribed a certain magical drink but unfortunately the poor child died after taking it.

The trial, if one could call it a trial, lasted six days, during which the accused confessed that she had frequently conversed with the fairy folk, had practised the forbidden Evil Arts and had sworn allegiance to her lord and master, Satan. The unfortunate woman was, of course, found guilty and she was strangled then burned at the stake. Even if Isobel Haldane had in fact been a witch, it would appear that her only crime had been her desire to help her neighbours. Unfortunately, like many other innocent men and women, Isobel Haldane was the victim of misplaced religious fervour and sheer bigotry. She suffered her dreadful fate for one simple reason – she was considered to be 'different'!

The Witch of Argyll
In volume I of the *Justiciary Records of Argyll and The Isles 1664-1705* is recorded the trial and subsequent execution of a certain Jannet McNicoll. The trial took place on 16 October 1673

before a distinguished panel of magistrates and justices. According to the official records, Jannet McNicoll was accused of the 'hideous and abominable' crime of witchcraft. The pannell (accused person) was said to have 'shaken off all fear of god reverence and respect to his majestie's lawes and acts of parliament is guiltie and culpable of the foresaid vile and abominable crime of witch-craft.'

McNicoll was stated to have met and conversed with the Devil himself on Hallowday 1661. It was said that the Devil appeared to her in the likeness of a gross leper-faced man and that she entered into a compact covenant with him. The Devil promised her that she would never want for clothes or ornaments if she would only follow him, and Jannet McNicoll renounced her Christian baptism and was given a new name by the Devil, a witch name – 'Mary Lykeas'. It was further stated that she continually met and consulted with the Devil at a place called Butekey on the shores of Rothesay. It was also stated that a number of other notorious witches met at the same place, four of whom were arrested, convicted and sentenced to death. McNicoll was also arrested and confessed to being a witch.

She was imprisoned in the Tolbooth jail in Rothesay in 1662, but fearing that she would be executed along with the other accused she broke free from her chains and escaped. She then fled to Kilmarnock, where she remained for some 12 years practising her evil arts. Her fame as a witch spread and she was then apprehended and brought to trial. She was found guilty and sentenced to be strangled to death and her body to be burned at the gallows of Rothesay on Friday 24 October at 2 o'clock in the afternoon. Her goods and possessions were ordered to be forfeited.

The Witch of Balnagowan

The tale of the Witch of Balnagowan is a most curious story of Scottish witchcraft; curious, because it illustrates a most unusual method of cursing someone to death, a method that does not seem to appear anywhere else in the strange history of witch cursing. Katherine Munro, born Katherine Ross of Balnagowan, was born of high rank and became Lady Fowlis when she married the fifteenth baron of Fowlis, the chief of the warlike Clan of Munro. Lady Fowlis quarrelled with her stepson, Robert Munro, her husband's eldest son and determined to cause his death by any means at her disposal, intending that Robert Munro's widow would then marry her own brother, George Ross of Balnagowan. She was also determined that her own sister-in-law, the present Lady Balnagowan, would also die by whatever means had to be used. According to court records, Lady Fowlis attempted to carry out her evil intentions without even bothering to hide the fact that these would involve the use of witchcraft.

She gathered around her an infamous crew of hag-witches and a number of evil characters with unsavoury reputations, who made clay effigies of both Robert Munro and also Lady Balnagowan. They also brewed a poisonous drink so strong that when an unsuspecting page tasted it he instantly fell mortally ill. The witches then prepared a second earthen jar of the same deadly potion and Lady Fowlis sent her own nurse to hand it to Robert Munro. On her way in the dark the servant stumbled and fell and the jar was broken. For some reason the nurse decided to taste the spilt liquid; she died almost instantly. From that day onwards only rank grass would grow on the spot where the deadly liquid had been spilt, and sheep and cattle refused to graze there.

Frustrated in her evil intentions Lady Fowlis then proceeded to use the full and terrible powers of Elfland. Laskie Loncraft, an assistant hag-witch, was instructed to fashion two elf-arrowheads made of flint. Clay images made earlier of the two intended victims were then set up at the north end of Lady Fowlis's apartments. A second assistant hag-witch, a certain Christian Ross Malcolmson, then shot two arrow shafts at the clay images of Lady Balnagowan and a further three shafts at the image of Robert Munro. Both images were smashed and then, surprisingly, Lady Fowlis commanded that her weird assistants make new images.

Hector Munro, who was Lady Fowlis's own son-in-law, was also closely involved in a conspiracy against his brother-in-law. Being taken suddenly ill with an unknown disease he consulted the family soothsayer and was told that he would soon die. He was then told that his fate could be averted if the 'principal man of his own blood suffered death in his place'. By this was meant a certain George Munro, his half-brother (Lady Fowlis's son). Hector Munro then sent seven messengers over a period of time to summon George Munro to his deathbed. Eventually George Munro arrived and Hector, relying on the advice of a notorious witch called Marion MacIngarach and also the advice of his own foster-mother, Christian Neil Dalyell, received him in cold and icy silence. After an hour of this inhospitable treatment his brother said, 'How be'est thee?' After a moment Hector replied, 'The better now that you, George, have come to visit me,' then instantly relapsed into stony silence.

One night shortly afterwards, after the hour of midnight, the witch, Marion MacIngarach, and her strange accomplices went out carrying spades. In total silence they dug a grave not very far from the seaside and on a piece of land bounded by two landowners. They took care to dig the grave to the exact size of Hector Munro and once it was dug the earth was carefully laid aside. It was then agreed, in order to avoid suspicion, that the spell against George Munro be suspended.

In January 1588 Hector Munro was carried, with due ceremony and in a blanket, to the grave and laid inside it. The loose earth was then shovelled on top of him. Marion MacIngarach sat by the graveside and Christian Neil Dalyell then ran the length of nine ridges holding a small boy by the hand. When she arrived back at the grave, Christian demanded of Marion MacIngarach which victim she chose. MacIngarach replied that she chose Hector to live and George to die in his place. The weird incantation was then repeated three times. George died some 12 months later.

Marion MacIngarach was eventually made the keeper of Hector Munro's sheep, but he refused point-blank to present her when told to do so at the subsequent trial. At the end of the trial only a few inferior people were found guilty of the crime of witchcraft and they paid the inevitable penalty. Lady Fowlis and Hector Munro were found not guilty, which was hardly surprising as the jury was composed of people of vastly inferior rank. The jury also took into consideration that from January 1588 until April 1590, when George Munro died, was too long a time for witchcraft to be considered as a cause of death. There is little doubt, having studied the court records, that both Lady Fowlis and Hector Munro were guilty of murder, or at least attempted murder, but as is so often the case, the guilty parties escaped scot-free with a few unfortunate scapegoats paying the penalty for their crimes.

Satans Invisible

WORLD

DISCOVERED;

O R,

A Choice Collection of Modern Relations, proving evidently against the *Saducees* and *Atheists* of this present Age, that there are *Devils*, *Spirits*, *Witches*, and *Apparitions*, from Authentick Records, Attestations of Famous Witnesses, and undoubted Verity.

To all which is added,

That Marvellous History of *Major Weir*, and his Sister:

With two Relations of Apparitions at *Edinburgh*.

By Mr *George Sinclar*, late Professor of Philosophy, in the Colledge of *Glasgow*.

No Man should be vain that he can injure the merit of a Book, for, the meanest Rogue may burn a City, or kill an Hero, whereas, he could never build the one, or equal the other. Sr. G. McK.

Edinburgh, Printed by *John Reid*. 1685.

2 Wizards and sorcerers

Major Weir

The practice of witchcraft and magic was not confined solely to the poor or middle class in Scotland, but was just as prevalent among the upper classes.

Major Thomas Weir was Commander of the Edinburgh City Guards and was known and highly respected throughout Edinburgh as a devout and extremely God-fearing lay preacher. Many of the city's richest and most respected families considered it a tremendous honour if he agreed to conduct a private prayer-meeting in their own homes. Dressed entirely in black, grim of countenance and always given to the old-fashioned habit of wearing a cloak, Major Weir's figure was a familiar sight in the cobbled streets of Edinburgh. He and his sister, Grizel or Jean, as she was sometimes known, lived alone in an old house in the West Bow and Grizel soon made a reputation for herself as being an expert spinner.

Weir belonged to the Bowhead Saints, an extremely strict Puritanical branch of the Presbyterians. He had an almost fanatical dislike of orthodox ministers and would scowl fiercely at them whenever he passed them in the street. Then suddenly rumours began to spread throughout the taverns and coffee-houses of the city, ugly rumours of witchcraft, magic and Devil worship. It was said that unless he held his curiously carved walking-stick the preacher was not quite so eloquent in his prayers. People whispered that they had never seen him kneel while praying. The rumours grew thick and fast and, of course, lost nothing in the telling. Terrified citizens told how they had often seen, late at night, Major Weir and his sister travelling down the High Street in a black coach drawn by six headless horses enveloped in blue flickering flames. Neighbours spoke of hearing unearthly noises coming from the preacher's house and told, with appropriate bated breath, of strange will-o'-the wisp lights being seen through the grimy windows. It was said that even when the house was known to be empty the sound of a spinning-wheel had been heard late at night.

Townspeople vied one with another to relate tales of sorcery and there were those who spoke of seeing weird beast-like shapes entering and leaving the house. Soon the stories reached incredible

proportions; it was believed that people climbing the stairs leading to his house found themselves going downwards. It was said that a strong smell of brimstone followed Major Weir wherever he went and some even said that they had seen his stick marching down the High Street in front of the sorcerer carrying a lantern to light his way at night.

Soon the tales came to the ears of the town's officials, who at first tried to disregard them, but suddenly, at a prayer-meeting, Major Weir himself confessed that he and his sister were both servants of the Devil. Weir confessed to so many hideous crimes that eventually the Lord Provost sent his own doctors to examine the self-confessed witch. When the doctors returned they declared that the preacher was quite sane but obviously suffering from a guilty conscience.

On 9 April 1670 Major Weir was arrested and charged with having committed incest with his sister, adultery with his step-daughter, Margaret Burden, and bestiality with different animals. Although sorcery and witchcraft were not included in the formal charges brought against him they were obviously taken for granted. His sister was charged with incest and sorcery and of being in league with those who consulted with the Devil.

At his trial Weir confessed that in his younger days he had made a pact with the Devil and that after he had received lessons in the art of sorcery he had also been given an extremely strange warning. It seems that Satan had warned him to beware of the word 'burn' because his death would be connected with this word. According to Weir the Devil had promised to protect him from all harm except anything connected with the dread word 'burn'. Weir never forgot this strange warning and once when he was making a tour of inspection of the City Guards he startled his officers by suddenly rushing away when he found out that one of the sentries at the Nether Bow Port was called Burn. On another day he arrived by accident at Liberton Burn and trembling violently he turned back and refused point-blank to go any further.

The Devil's strange and ominous warning came true on 11 April 1670 when, at the age of seventy-one, the once highly respected lay preacher was burned alive at the Gallow Hill. A vast crowd gathered to watch the infamous sorcerer meet his just deserts and a cheer went up when his magic stick was thrown into the flames beside its owner. The stick, with its carved satyr heads, was said to twist and turn as though trying to avoid the hungry flames and onlookers even said that it screamed aloud in hellish agony. Grizel was hanged on the following day at the Grassmarket and the unfortunate creature struggled violently all the way to the scaffold.

Major Weir's house stood empty for over a century and local residents were firmly convinced that evil spirits haunted the ill-fated building. At night hideous laughter and wild unearthly shrieks could be heard and strange wraith-like apparitions could be seen through the broken windows. It was also believed that late at night Major Weir's ghost frequently galloped up and down the High Street, mounted on a black headless horse with the ghastly flames of Hell surrounding both horse and rider. Finally, in 1878, the building was demolished and only the legend remained, a legend that still persists, however, to this very day.

Alexander Skene

Peter Pan is not the only legendary character who had the misfortune to lose his shadow; this also happened to Alexander Skene, a young Scottish nobleman.

Skene went to Italy some time in the seventeenth century to study the Black Arts and he apparently spent seven years there learning his infernal trade from none other than the Devil himself.

On his last night in Italy, having qualified as a master wizard, Skene and his fellow pupils were told that it was now time to pay their agreed fees. The Devil informed them that it was his time-honoured custom to take the soul of the last pupil leaving his classroom. Needless to say there was an instant rush to leave the Devil's presence and Skene had the misfortune to be the last from the room. The Devil seized him but the young Scottish nobleman tricked him by calling out, 'There is one more behind me, Master, seize him!' and the Devil immediately released him and seized, not another pupil but Skene's shadow.

Alexander Skene returned to Skene House, his ancestral home, about 10 miles west of Aberdeen and there he became known as the 'Wizard Laird'. It was said that even in the brightest sunlight, he never cast the slightest hint of a shadow. Skene was always accompanied on his travels abroad by four familiars or imps – a hawk, a magpie, a crow and a jackdaw. These strange companions would sit beside their master in a ghostly coach drawn by black headless horses and without riders. The local graveyard was usually their destination and once there Skene would open the graves and remove the bodies of unbaptised babies, which provided a grisly feast for his four unholy companions.

Night after night, always on the final stroke of midnight, the Wizard Laird visited neighbouring glens searching for rare herbs to use in his magical potions. It is clear that Skene intensely disliked any form of magical competition, for apparently he frequently used his weird poisonous concoctions to get rid of rival witches.

According to an old legend, Skene used to cross the Loch of Skene in his coach in winter, supported only by his magical powers, although the loch was only covered by a thin layer of ice. He always attempted this feat on the last night of the year and his coachman was instructed to have the coach ready by midnight. One year there was no frost so Skene used his magical powers to cast a thin layer of ice over the surface of the loch. The Wizard Laird instructed his coachman to keep the horses at full gallop during the crossing. The coachman was also warned that he must never turn his head to look behind him. That night the coach thundered across the thin ice while Skene's four weird companions flew ahead and Skene himself kept muttering strange incantations. Finally the horses reached the other side and the terrified coachman, almost beside himself with terror, forgot his strict instructions and turned round. To his horror there beside the laird sat the Devil himself. Instantly the back wheels of the coach crashed through the thin ice and two enormous black hounds who had been following the coach plunged into the icy, dark waters of the loch. It is said that the Wizard Laird merely shook his head sadly at the terrified coachman and then he and the Devil returned safely to Skene House.

Alexander Hunter

East Lothian seems to have held a particular fascination for Satan in days gone by and His Infernal Majesty appears to have been kept extremely busy teaching his many eager followers the curious tricks of his unholy trade.

One of the most famous or perhaps infamous wizards in East Lothian was a cattle-herder by the name of Alexander Hunter. Hunter specialised in curing diseases by means of spells and charms and he cured both men and animals. He claimed that he

had met the Devil on a hillside outside Haddington and that the Devil had appeared to him in the shape of an old, learned physician.

The Devil had told Hunter that it was now time for him to acknowledge Satan as his master and that in return for this he would be taught the complete art of spells, conjuration and incantations. Hunter eagerly agreed and Satan then gave him the notorious Devil's mark together with a new name, a witch name – 'Hatteraick', a name by which he was thereafter known throughout the entire countryside. Soon Hatteraick became famous for his healing arts and there were very few people who would refuse to give him money or food, not because of his healing powers but because of his evil reputation for casting malevolent spells on those who incurred his displeasure by refusing to give him alms.

One day the brother of Lady Samuelston met him on the outskirts of Haddington and, being in a foul temper, struck the wizard across the face, calling him a 'warlock carle'. Hatteraick instantly cursed him and the nobleman, realising too late his folly, rode off deeply regretting his hasty action. It appears that he rode through a dark, deserted part of the countryside where he met a number of people whose strange and frightening appearance struck fear and trembling into his heart. When he eventually returned home he began to rant and rave and fell into a black brooding mood.

Guessing what had happened, his sister, Lady Samuelston, immediately sent servants to fetch the notorious sorcerer. When Hatteraick arrived he was given food and drink and was promised a large sum of gold if he would consent to remove the curse he had laid. Hatteraick demanded that one of the nobleman's shirts be brought to him and when he received it he carried out a curious occult ritual using the shirt. In a very short time the brother recovered but the sorcerer told Lady Samuelston that her brother would soon leave the country and would never return. It was widely known that Hatteraick's prophecies usually came true so Lady Samuelston persuaded her brother to sign over his share of the family's estate and income to her, thus defrauding his younger brother, George. Not long after this Hatteraick was arrested in Dunbar, taken to Edinburgh and tried on a charge of witchcraft. He was burned on the Castle Hill.

The horned god Cernunnos (an original sketch by Kevin Grimshaw from the author's collection)

William, Lord Soulis

Gilles de Rais was infamous in France as a dreaded sorcerer; his counterpart in Scotland was the notorious William, Lord Soulis who, according to legend, had sold his soul to the Devil. It appears that he indulged in almost every type of Black Magic and practised every known form of sorcery. He was reputed to be able to summon the cursed demon whenever he wished, by merely rapping three times on a certain iron chest. It was also said, however, that when he did so he must never look in the direction of the evil spirit. On one occasion he forgot this important proviso and saw, standing beside the iron chest, a huge dark man wearing a crimson cap stained with the blood of countless victims. Even though Soulis had broken his part of the contract it seems that Satan still kept his, but from that moment onwards the sorcerer's doom was sealed.

It appears that Lord Soulis was protected by a magical charm which ensured that he was safe from any injury or hurt caused by rope or steel, so that cords were unable to bind him nor could any sword pierce him. Eventually, however, when he was seized by his enemies, he was rolled up in several sheets of lead and then boiled alive at Nine-Stone Rig.

An ancient poem commemorates the celebrated death of the evil sorcerer:

> On a circle of stones they placed the pot,
> On a circle of stones but barely nine;
> They heated it red and fiery hot,
> And the burnished brass did glimmer and shine.
> They rolled him up in a sheet of lead -
> A sheet of lead for a funeral pall;
> They plunged him into the cauldron red,
> And melted him body, lead, bones and all.

Hermitage Castle, where the black magician carried out many of his evil deeds and orgies, was believed to have eventually sunk deep into the earth, unable, so it was said, to bear the heavy weight of his many infamies. Legend has it that every seven years the earthbound spirit of the ancient wizard still meets with his master, the Devil, in the dungeons of the old castle, where they are forced to re-enact their past evil deeds.

Other wizards and sorcerers

In 1629 an infamous sorcerer by the name of Alexander Hamilton was arrested on a charge of sorcery and of being in league with the Devil. While he was imprisoned in the Tolbooth, Hamilton accused nine Haddington women of also being in league with the Devil and of being witches. At his subsequent trial he confessed that the Devil himself had taught him the evil trade of Black Magic. He stated that Satan had first appeared to him on Kingston Hill in Haddingtonshire in the shape of a black man. Hamilton boasted that whenever he wanted the Devil to appear he would strike the ground three times with a fir stick, at the same time crying out 'Rise up, foul fiend.' Depending on his disposition at the time, the Devil would then appear as a large black crow, a dog or sometimes an enormous black cat. During his trial Hamilton implicated a number of other people as being in league with Satan. The sorcerer was found guilty and sentenced to be strangled at the stake, then burned.

At one time a notorious wizard lived in the Shetlands, a curious individual known to the local inhabitants as 'Luggie'. According to local legend whenever Luggie was hungry he would put out to sea, cast his line into the water and then bring out boiled or roasted fish. If at any time during the year the storms were too severe to put out to sea this particular follower of the Devil would climb a high hill near his house then cast his fishing-line into a deep pit. After pronouncing certain strange and powerful incantations the wizard would then draw up an amazing variety of edible fish. Despite his undoubted skill as a fisherman, albeit a somewhat strange one, Luggie was eventually executed as a wizard.

Even the great reformer, John Knox, was accused by Catholics of being a wizard of some repute: it was said that he attempted to raise several spirits in the churchyard of St Andrews, and that Satan himself appeared with a huge pair of horns on his head; terrified at the dreadful sight Knox's secretary went mad and died.

3 Spells and curses

Curses

Amongst their many strange powers, witches were believed to have the ability to curse their enemies. There were many curious and terrible ways in which an intended victim could be cursed. At one time it was firmly believed that the victim had to know that he or she was being cursed before the curse could become effective. However, recent research has revealed that, strangely enough, there have been numerous cases where the victim was totally unaware that he or she was the focus of evil and destructive forces. Obviously, from a purely psychological point of view, if the victim knows that he or she is being cursed then subconscious forces can soon achieve the desired effect, but throughout the history of witchcraft there have been many instances where an unsuspecting victim has been crippled, blinded or even killed, as the direct result of an evil curse.

Even after recognising that witches were quite capable of using poisons and drugs in order to achieve their evil ends an element of 'magic' still exists. One of the most ancient and particularly virulent methods of cursing was the notorious 'Evil Eye'. This type of cursing required no form of speech and has been recognised all over the world. It was sometimes known as 'The Art of Fascination' or 'Binding by the Look or Sight'. Another term for it was 'overlooking' and it was frequently used by witches to bewitch cattle or other farm animals. As recently as 1927, for instance, there is the story of a certain 'wise woman' who was ridiculed by farm workers (who should have known better, as the old woman was well known in the district as being a witch). Without saying a word, the wise woman glared at the farm tractor as it slowly chugged its way across a field. It stopped immediately and even a mechanic from the nearby village garage failed to rectify or even find the fault, if indeed there was one.

In the Scottish Highlands it was once and, who knows, perhaps still is to this very day firmly believed that should a stranger praise a fine cow too strongly and also keep gazing at the animal that the unfortunate creature would slowly waste away. This was believed to be the direct result of the Evil Eye and the spell could only be broken by immediately offering the stranger some of the animal's milk to drink.

In many witch trials it was confessed by the accused that Satan himself had given his disciples a certain method of cursing, for instance it might be said that the Lord of Evil had told his followers that if they bore ill will or malice towards anybody, all they had to do was to carry out the following instructions: 'Look at them with open eyes and pray evil for them in my name and you will achieve your heart's desire.'

In Isabel Cameron's delightful and fascinating book, A Highland Chapbook, there is a description of the powers possessed by a witch who had the ability to cast the Evil Eye: she

> Could o'ercast the night, and cloud the moon
> And mak' the deils obedient to her crune,
> At midnight hours o'er the kirkyards she raves
> And howks unchristened weans out of their graves;
> Boils up their livers in a warlock's pow;
> And seven times does her prayers backwards pray;
> Then mix't with venom of black tiads and snakes.
> Of this unsousy pictures aft she makes
> Of ony she hates; – and gars expire
> With shaw and racking pains afore a fire;
> Stuck full of pines the devlish pictures melt;
> The pain by fowk they represent is felt.
> Whilst she and cat sit beeking in her yard...

Needless to say, there were also various counter-charms or spells to ward off the effects of the dreaded Evil Eye. It was once believed that to be seized with an unexpected fit of yawning meant that an enemy was casting the Evil Eye upon you. In order to avert the curse the bewitched person was required immediately to pronounce the following counter-spell:

> The eye that goes over me and through me,
> The eye that pierces to the bone and the marrow,
> I will overthrow and the elements will help me.

One of the most effective counter-charms against the Evil Eye was to make the 'Cornus Manatu' – an ancient charm well known in ancient Babylon and Egypt. This was carried out by instantly doubling the thumb in the right hand and then protruding the first and fourth finger to make the infamous 'Devil's Horn'. One must remember that according to ancient occult laws if a curse is

thwarted it immediately rebounds and reverts back on the person who originally uttered it. This explains why ancient and modern sorcerers always use a 'medium' through whom they direct their evil spells; should the spell be rebounded the unfortunate 'medium' will then suffer the inevitable result and the sorcerer will escape scot-free.

In Scotland, one of the most popular cures for having been bewitched by the Evil Eye was known as 'burn airgid'. This was water into which gold or silver coins, especially silver, had been placed. It had to be lifted in a wooden ladle from a running stream over which both the living and the dead had passed. It was then blessed in the name of the Trinity, the sign of the cross was made over it and a certain rhyme was repeated.

Horseshoes have always been considered to be extremely lucky, but only if they are nailed to a wall or door with the open points upwards. The reason for this is to ensure that the good luck does not run out of the open ends, although it is also said that the horseshoe is placed this way because it represents the Devil's horns. The same lucky horseshoe is said to be extremely effective against the powers of the Evil Eye.

According to legend the Devil once entered a certain blacksmith's forge somewhere in the Highlands and asked to be shod. The actual shoeing was so painful, however, that the Devil begged the blacksmith to cease, but the wily old smith refused, until eventually the Devil agreed that he would meet any conditions the blacksmith imposed if he would only stop his painful work. The blacksmith made him promise that neither the Devil nor any of his followers would ever enter a building which had a horseshoe nailed over the threshold.

Apart from the Evil Eye, witches used many other forms of cursing. To cause an animal to cease giving milk, for example, the witch would plait a length of tow the wrong way (widdershin, i.e. against the movement of the sun or anti-clockwise) then draw the cord beneath the cow's feet. In order to remove the strength from an enemy's ale, mould from the local graveyard was placed beneath the house door. If the mould had been thrown up by a mole so much the better. The witch's enemy would then be left with pure water whilst the witch herself obtained the strength of the ale in her own home-brew. Witches were also notorious for magically removing honey from the hive, corn from the ear of the sheaf and

Miniature coffins found on Arthur's Seat, Edinburgh (National Museum of Antiquities of Scotland)

fish from the fisherman's net. They were also said to be able to take the colour out of the dyeing vat (except for black which, being Satan's own special colour, was immune).

One of the commonest and most virulent forms of witchcraft cursing was the making of a waxen moppet – a poppet or wax doll baptised in the name of a human being. It was said that whatever happened to the wax doll would automatically happen to the human being whose name the doll bore. The doll (known in Gaelic as the *corp criadh*) was formed of clay or wax, and pins, rusty nails and needles would be thrust into it. To be really effective, nail parings and clippings of hair taken from the intended victim were also moulded into the waxen figure. A baptism ceremony was then carried out and after that the witch began her evil work in deadly earnest. Additional nails or needles would be thrust into the doll to increase the pain, until the witch was satisfied that her intended victim was writhing in mortal agony. The doll was then buried in the ground or placed into a running stream. As it crumbled or melted away, so, it was believed, would the victim. Sometimes the doll was placed in front of a fire and basted with ale, so that as the wax melted the human being would slowly waste away, dying eventually from what we would now call consumption.

Practitioners of witchcraft who had attained a very high standard in their evil arts frequently used 'moon paste', especially effective when used in Black Magic ceremonies. This was made by 'pulling the moon from the sky': certain herbs had to be pounded and mixed whilst the moon was full, then water was taken from seven different wells and the whole mixture was kneaded in a trough in a churchyard with suitable chanting and continual 'widdershin' turnings. It was said that images made of this particular paste were capable of bringing woe and disaster on anyone the witch wished to curse.

A particularly nasty form of cursing was the affliction of erysipelas, which the witch achieved by cutting snippets of red hair then scattering them with suitable cursing in the direction of her enemy; each snippet of hair touching the intended victim would become a festering sore.

Should a witch for some reason take a dislike to a newly married couple then he or she would pronounce the following dreadful curse: 'May you have no son to succeed you!' A certain rite was performed with due ceremony during the uttering of this particular curse. A cake was baked using corn or meal magically stolen from other villagers. It was kneaded widdershin and a hole made in the centre of it, then the waxen image of a small child was passed through the hole. The doll was passed through three times, backwards and forwards, whilst the evil one muttered certain mystical words.

Witches also might put curses on children using the special spell known as 'forspoken', described in the next section, 'Spells and incantations'.

The story of Helen Rogie, known as the 'Witch of Findrack', shows how witches could use their powers for curses. She belonged to a notorious witch coven which regularly met near Torphins, and was arrested after uttering curses against a certain wealthy farmer, John Mackie, and his family. Mrs Mackie fell and broke her leg and one of Mackie's daughters suddenly died, while some time earlier the Mackies' dog had mysteriously passed away after trying to bite the witch-wife. Various other strange mishaps befell the Mackies' neighbours and eventually the assizes were persuaded to issue a warrant for her arrest. Somehow, however, Helen Rogie received advance information that she was about to be taken into custody and promptly fled to safety.

For several days she managed to avoid being captured but eventually she was traced to a secret cave in the nearby hills. Before she was captured the arresting officers had searched her cottage and there they discovered a large number of images fashioned out of soft lead, curious writings and numerous pieces of twisted wire and coloured threads. At her subsequent trial in 1597 it was agreed that the accused woman be taken to the Gallows Hill at Craigour and there be burned alive. The court also agreed that the following expenses be deducted from her estate: '66 pence to pay for the district hangman and sufficient funds to cover the expenses of twenty loads of peat, a boll of coal, four barrels of tar, four lengths of strong rope and – a stake.'

A particularly interesting form of witch cursing is described in the story of Lady Fowlis, 'The Witch of Balnagowan', told in chapter 1 of this book, 'Famous witches'.

Spells and incantations
Many stories told about Scottish witches give details of their skill in casting spells. Straw, for instance, often played an important

part in both good and evil spells. If a witch wanted to drive someone insane, he or she would throw a wisp of straw in that person's face, while the notorious Scottish witch, Isobel Gowdie (see chapter 1, 'Famous witches'), who had been taught her dark practices by none other than Satan himself, was believed to be able to change a windle-straw into a horse. Dorothy Calder, the witch from Forres, frequently helped the salmon fishers of the Findhorn to make a good haul by tying a circle of knotted straw round their waists then chanting a certain old spell. Having done this she would tell the men to go out fishing – they would be sure to make a good catch. She warned them, however, 'that ye'll get one "gleyed" one; dinna tak him, put him back in a pool, he's the de'il!'

Witches frequently bespelled children if they held a grudge against the parents. This particular form of cursing was known as 'forspoken' and it was extremely effective. In order to bespell or 'forspeak' children, witches used black wool and butter together with a peculiar chant.

Janet Traill, another famous Scottish witch, confessed that she had several times been ordered by the fairy folk to cast spells bringing ill to various people but that she had always refused. According to her court confession she stated that green yarn was often used in the practice of black magic. Sometimes if a witch wished to bring illness to someone she would cut a length of green yarn into nine pieces then bury the various pieces in the lands of three lairds.

Among the numerous tales of the evil doings of witches in the Orkney and Shetland Islands is one about a certain witch well known in the parish of Dunrossness, who was a sworn enemy of the skipper and crew of a local fishing vessel. When the fishing boat went sailing one fine cloudless day, the witch, who was watching from her cottage, decided to destroy it by raising a magical storm. She took a small wooden basin (known locally as a 'cap') and placed it in a tub of water, then, going back indoors, she began to recite an ancient Norse chant and carried on with her housework. After a few moments she sent her child out to tell her what was happening to the basin floating in the tub of water. The child returned to tell her that the water in the tub was becoming increasingly disturbed but that the 'cap' was still floating peacefully on the surface. Infuriated, the witch chanted louder and louder and once more told her child to inform her of the progress of the wooden basin. Again

Old Mother Longnose, a legendary Edinburgh witch (The Witchery Restaurant, Edinburgh)

the child told her mother that whilst the water in the tub was becoming even more disturbed the wooden 'cap' was still floating peacefully. With increased fervour the witch, who was almost demented by this time, screamed the ancient chant louder and louder and then suddenly the wooden 'cap' capsized. With a loud and frenzied shriek the witch exclaimed, 'The turn is done!' She then ceased chanting and collapsed, exhausted, into a rocking-chair. The fishing boat capsized and all its crew, including the skipper, perished.

Although witches were normally associated with causing harm by means of their diabolic spells, there were many occasions when they worked their magic solely in order to achieve good and often without any thought of payment apart, perhaps, from a little meat, butter and cheese. Both Bessie Dunlop and Alison Pearson (see chapter 6) were such witches and another example of a witch working good can be found in the folklore of Tynron in Dumfries.

An old farmer told how a witch had once helped him when he was a young boy carting stone from a quarry. His horse had come to a sudden standstill outside the house of a well-known local witch and two carters passing by had jeered and laughed sarcastically at both the witch and the young boy. The witch, to whom the boy had always been polite on previous occasions, came forward and with a slight push adjusted a heavy stone which had slipped from the cart and jammed one of the wheels. 'Now, go,' she said, 'Thou wilt find them at the gate below Gilchristland.' Sure enough the boy found the two perplexed carters standing, both their horses sweating and trembling, at the very spot indicated by the witch. It was many hours before the two carters returned to their village.

Another interesting case, this time of magical healing, occurred in the year 1708 in the Orkney Islands. William Stensgar of Southside in Orkney was struck by a sudden and extremely pain-ful attack of rheumatism, and eventually, in sheer desperation sought the aid of a witch or beggar woman known locally as Catherine Taylor. The 'wise woman' told him that he must accom-pany her to a certain stile at sunrise on the following morning. Both Stensgar and his wife set out the next morning, his wife carrying, according to the witch's instructions, a pail of water. Once they reached the stile the witch rubbed Stensgar's afflicted knee and, at the same time, recited first a strange magical incantation and then the Twenty-third Psalm. To his astonishment Stensgar realised that the rheumatism had completely vanished and that his knee was now free from pain. The witch then told the delighted couple that the illness had been magically transferred into the pail of water. His wife was ordered to empty the pail of water over the stile so that the next person crossing it would be immediately afflicted with the illness. A local man who had followed the strange trio and watched the curious ceremony from a distance avoided the illness by walking past the stile. However, some time later, another local inhabitant was unlucky enough to step over the stile and was instantly laid low with the transferred illness – rheumatism!

One of the strangest of old tales concerns the Spanish Armada and comes from the Island of Mull. During a violent storm a Spanish galleon was blown ashore and wrecked and the body of an unfortunate Spanish princess was washed ashore on the sandy beach. The inhabitants of the island hastily buried the body but without the benefit of Christian burial. Because of this, local superstition had it that the dead stranger, unable to lie in peace, was condemned to haunt the island for ever.

On learning of the tragedy, the king of Spain ordered that a ship be sent to the island at once with the intent of avenging his daughter's death. The ship was to be commanded by a certain Captain Forrest, a skilled sailor and a man well versed in the dreaded 'Black Arts'. Forrest proudly boasted that he would 'sweep the entire Island of Mull bare and lay it waste, sparing none of the heathen inhabitants'. The islanders were naturally terrified at this threat and immediately sought the aid of the famous (or infamous) witches of Mull.

These particular 'wise women', known as the 'Doideagan Muileach', all gathered speedily in one particular place and the Lord of Duart himself implored them to raise a terrible wind – a wind that would sink the Spanish ship. With one accord the witches asked if the said Captain Forrest had been bold enough to say 'With God's help I will sweep and destroy the island'. Duart replied, 'He did not say with God's help,' whereupon one of the witches said, 'Good is that, his end is nigh!'

She tied a straw rope to a quern-stone then passed the rope over the rafters of a nearby house, and raised the quern-stone as high as she could. As the stone rose so did a tremendous wind. Owing, however, to the counter-spells of Captain Forrest, the witch was unable to raise the millstone any higher. In desperation she screamed to her sister witches to help her and they rushed to her assistance, but even with their combined strength the unholy crew was unable to move the stone any higher. The first witch then begged the strongest man on the island, Domhnull Dubh Laidir (Black Donald the Strong) to come to their aid. Even Black Donald, however, with all his mighty strength, could do no more than hold the stone in position; he was totally unable to raise it.

Amongst the island's witches only one had failed to attend the gathering. Gormal of Mull was missing and a deputation was despatched in haste to implore her to come to their aid. When Gormal finally arrived she grasped the straw rope and with one tremendous effort heaved on it. Up went the quern-stone, up rose the storm and a howling wind screamed its way around the island. Down went the Spanish galleon, and Captain Forrest and his Spanish crew were buried for ever in the depths of the bay. An old Mull song commemorates the feat.

Aha! Captain Forrest, thou didst boast
Last year to desolate Mull's coast,
But now, Hoo-hoo! thy ship is lost!

When one reads stories such as this of the vengeance of witches, it is little wonder that they were held in fear and dread.

Grimoires

Throughout the long history of witchcraft in Scotland, it has been rumoured that witches, wizards and necromancers had frequent recourse to certain forbidden and dangerous 'Books of Spells', usually known as grimoires. One of the most famous, or perhaps infamous, of these notorious books was the Red Book of Appin. This incredible book was known to have been in existence as recently as the year 1825, and was believed to have been stolen from none other than the Devil himself by means of a clever trick. It was said to contain a large number of magical runes as well as various incantations to cure the diseases of cattle, and also spells to increase flocks and methods to ensure the fertility of crops. The book was last heard of as being in the possession of the now extinct family of the Stewarts of Invernahyle. It was believed that possession of this dreaded volume conferred dark and evil powers upon its owner: whoever possessed it would know beforehand what questions would be asked and, more important, the answers the enquirer wished to have. The book was believed to be so powerful that whoever read it was required to wear a band of iron round his or her forehead before turning the mystic pages.

One of the most famous stories about magical writings must be that of Tarquin the Proud, legendary King of Rome, and the Sibylline books. It dates from about 534 BC when King Tarquin was visited one day by a mysterious old woman. She was of grave and venerable appearance and entered the royal palace without even being stopped or questioned by the guards. Holding out nine ancient books, she offered them, at a price, to King Tarquin. The sum she asked was so high, however, that the King laughed in scorn and ordered her to leave the palace immediately. The old woman turned and threw three of the books into a flaming brazier then watched, in complete silence, as they burned. When nothing remained of the books but ashes she offered the remaining six books to the King at the same price as before. Again laughing scornfully the King said, 'You wish me to buy six books for the same price as nine books. You must be mad. Get you hence.'

Once more the ancient hag threw three books into the all-consuming flames. Again she held out the remaining books and once more offered them at the original price. This time King Tarquin purchased the books and having paid the required price watched as the old woman silently left his palace. She was never seen again.

When the King and his priests examined the books they found that they contained a tremendous amount of magical lore and strange prophecies, and with great reverence they were laid upon the shrine of Jupiter in the temple devoted to his worship. It was later believed that the old woman had been the Sibyl of Cumae.

Throughout the following centuries many strange books of spells and magical lore were handed down from magician to magician. One of the oldest and most terrible books ever written was the *Sepher Toldos Jeschu* – a Syro-Chaldaic book on sorcery – the contents of which were mercifully understood by only a few human beings, while one of the most infamous books of darkest necromancy was the *Marvellous Secrets of Albert the Great*. It was believed that this learned book had been written by the Dominican Bishop of Cologne, St Albert the Great, who died in 1280. A second book, *Le Petit Albert, Rare and Cabbalistic Secrets of Albert the Less* ('Le Petit Albert'), was later published and was said to have been compiled by Alberto Lucio Minore. Each of these extremely rare tracts has been republished at various times but the first editions have long been rare collectors' items.

The list of grimoires is almost endless and many of these have been reprinted in modern times. They include the *Book of Sacred Magic*, said to have been written and compiled by Moses himself when he was on Mount Sinai.

There are hundreds more of these famous 'Books of Spells', a few of which are listed below:

The Sixth and Seventh Book of Moses
Albertus Magnus or *White and Black Arts for Men and Beasts*
The Great Book of Black Magic
The Black Art Bible
The Art of Moses
The Grimoire of Pope Honorius
The Sworn Book of Honorius III
Clavicula Solomonis ('The Key of Solomon the King') or
   Book of the Pentacles
The Keys of Rabbi Solomon
The Black Book of Agrippa
The Elements of Magic of Pietro d'Abano
The True and Only Key of King Solomon
Solomon's Key
Magia de Profundis
Zekerboni

In addition, one must not forget the 'Book of Shadows', which every witch was said to own. This was a collection of spells and incantations, with recipes for the concoction of drugs and poisons and a list of members of the witch's own particular coven. The 'Book of Shadows' was always handwritten by the witch herself.

4 Witch cats

It was commonly believed that every witch possessed a familiar, an imp or demon in the shape of a small animal, usually a toad. The familiar fed on the witch's blood and was sent by her to attack her enemies or to carry messages to other members of the coven. Witches were also said to be experts at shape changing and there are numerous instances of witches taking on the form or appearance of a cat.

The Edinburgh Council Minutes record that in 1611 a known witch, Barbara Mylne, was seen by a certain Janet Allan, who herself was burned for witchcraft, to enter by the Water Gate in the 'likeness of a catt, and did change her garments under her own staire and then enter her house'.

In 1607 in the small mining village of Prestonpans, East Lothian, lived a certain Isobel Grierson who was married to John Bull, a labourer. It appears that Isobel was regarded by her neighbours as a somewhat vindictive and extremely quarrelsome woman, always arguing with people and forever bearing grudges. Eventually someone accused her of being a witch and of being in league with Satan and she was arrested and brought to trial.

The court was told that she had bewitched and cast spells on an Adam Clark of Prestonpans for over a year and a half. One winter's night in November 1606, when Adam Clark and his wife were in bed, Isobel Grierson crept into the house in the shape of a large cat and, accompanied by a number of other cats, proceeded to terrorise the frightened couple. A serving-woman in the household was attacked by the Devil in the guise of a black man who dragged the unfortunate woman around the house before disappearing in a cloud of black sulphurous smoke. Not surprisingly the poor woman fell ill as a result of her dreadful experience and was confined to bed for six weeks.

As the trial proceeded, more and more incredible incidents were related and the magistrates were told that she had quarrelled with a William Burnet, also of Prestonpans, and that the said William Burnet had been stricken with a fearful sickness because of a piece of raw, enchanted meat cast into his house by the accused. Satan himself, in the shape of a small naked child, appeared every night and stood in front of the fire holding a wax doll. Isobel Grierson also haunted the house and appeared in numerous fearful shapes and terrorised the occupants by carrying out various acts of evil maliciousness. Only when William Burnet called out the witch's name did the apparitions vanish, but Burnet lay ill for over three years and eventually died from a slow wasting illness.

Another neighbour, one Robert Peddan, fell ill and became subject to strange fainting fits which the doctors were unable to cure. It was only when Peddan remembered that he owed Grierson a certain sum of money that he realised that he was under a spell of enchantment. Strangely enough after he had repaid the money due he was cured of his mysterious illness within 24 hours.

It was also believed that Isobel Grierson had cast a spell causing ale brewing in various vats to become foul and evil-smelling, thus ruining the brewer's livelihood.

The accused was not allowed any defence and as the sole witnesses at her trial were Adam Clark, William Burnet's widow and Robert Peddan and his wife it is hardly surprising that the court brought in the usual verdict of guilty. Isobel Grierson was taken to the Castle Hill and was there 'strangled at the stake until she was dead, her body was burned to ashes and the ashes were thrown to the winds'. Her entire estate was handed over to the Crown and the good people of Prestonpans heaved a sigh of relief that another follower of Satan had paid the penalty.

Another very curious example of a witch's power to change into a cat took place in 1718 at Thurso in Caithness. The witch was known as Margaret Nin-Gilbertson and one day her friend, Margaret Olsen, was evicted from her house by her landlord, a man called Fraser. Fraser rented the house to a certain William Montgomery and Olsen asked her witch friend to cast a spell upon her landlord.

For some reason the witch's spells failed to take effect and so she decided to try them on the new tenant, Montgomery. Shortly afterwards Montgomery's house became so overrun with cats of all shapes and sizes that it became unsafe for his family to remain there. Montgomery himself was actually away on business at the time but his wife sent messengers to him five times warning him that unless he returned to protect his family they would flee to Thurso. The family's servant left them suddenly when one night five of the cats crouched beside the fireplace and talked to each other in human voices.

Montgomery arrived home prepared to do battle with the strange intruders and that night he and his assistant, William

Geddes, caught one cat, drove a dirk through its body, beat it with a sword then threw it out as dead. The following morning the body had vanished. A few nights later the army of cats came back and again the two men managed to catch a cat in a plaid, stabbed it several times then smashed its head in with an axe. Again the body was thrown out and again it had vanished in the morning.

Realising that witchcraft was at work, Montgomery reported the entire affair to the sheriff depute at Caithness and asked if any person of ill repute had fallen sick or been found wounded. It was reported that Margaret Gilbertson had been seen by a neighbour to drop one of her legs at her own front door. The black and putrefied leg was brought before the sheriff depute.

Gilbertson was at once arrested and immediately confessed that she was in league with the Devil whom, she said, often appeared to her in the shape of a huge black cloud. She also admitted to having been at Montgomery's house in the form of a cat and that she had been so severely struck with a dirk that after reaching her own home one of her legs had fallen off. She implicated various other women including her friend Olsen and said that all of them had taken the shape of cats. Gilbertson died in prison some weeks later, her friend Olsen was pricked (see chapter 7, 'Witch-prickers') and the inevitable Devil's mark was found on her body. Strangulation and burning was, of course, her fate and from then on Montgomery was no longer troubled by cats or witches.

Another strange tale of shape changing occurred in Jedburgh in the year 1752. Captain Archibald Douglas and an army sergeant were touring the Border district on a recruiting mission. The Sergeant complained to Douglas that his billet was haunted and that he had found out that his landlord possessed the power of second sight, while his landlady was reputed to be a notorious witch. Eventually Douglas agreed to spend the night in the haunted cottage in order to discover whether there was any truth in his Sergeant's complaints. On the stroke of midnight an enormous black cat leapt through the window and Captain Douglas promptly fired his pistol at the animal, shooting off one of its ears. The cat screamed in a human fashion and instantly vanished. The following morning the Captain discovered the landlady lying on the floor of the kitchen; her head was covered in blood and one of her ears was missing.

A Highland laird once discovered that his wine kept on disappearing mysteriously and, being convinced that it could only be due to witchcraft, he decided to catch the culprits redhanded. Arming himself with a broadsword he descended to his wine cellar late one night. To his astonishment he found himself surrounded by dozens of cats of all shapes and sizes. With a wild yell the laird laid about him with his broadsword and the cats fled in all directions. Drops of blood on the flagstones showed that he had struck at least one of the strange cats. Next day the laird and some of the servants searched the house of a notorious local witch. The old woman was found in bed with one of her legs completely severed.

Over 300 years ago there lived a famous hunter who was reputed to fear neither man nor the Devil and his entire life was devoted to ridding Badenoch and the surrounding district of witches and Devil-worshippers. According to the legend the hunter was out late one evening with his hunting-dogs when a terrible storm arose. So ferocious was the storm that the hunter was forced to take shelter in a herdsman's deserted cottage. He had just lit a fire when he heard a tremendous scratching at the door and when he opened it he found a bedraggled cat cowering against the wall. Calling off his dogs the hunter carried the cat into the hut and began to dry its soaking bedraggled fur. Then, to his utter astonishment, the animal spoke to him and told him that she was a witch come to seek his aid in an attempt to mend her evil ways.

The cat then asked the hunter to tie up his dogs to an overhead beam and gave him a long grey hair to use as a rope. Naturally enough the wily hunter was somewhat suspicious of the witch and only pretended to tie up his hounds by fastening only one end of the long hair to the beam.

Suddenly the cat began to grow in size then swiftly changed into a woman, whom the hunter recognised as being a neighbour from his village in Inverness. The hunter was more than surprised to recognise the witch because she was considered to be an extremely virtuous woman and was so highly respectable that she was known as the 'Goodwife of Laggan'. The witch suddenly gave vent to a shrieking hideous laugh then hissed, 'O famous Hunter of the Hills, be ready to die. This morning I drowned our greatest persecutor in Raasay. Now it is your turn to perish!' The witch leapt at the hunter, her hooked fingers clawing desperately and viciously at his throat. Barking fiercely his hounds leapt at her and the old witch screamed 'Fasten, fasten!' whereupon the hair tightened so hard on the beam that the wood split asunder. The terrified dogs tore at the old woman's flesh and unable to beat them off she changed instantly into a raven and flew out through a window.

When the storm finally abated the hunter returned home to find his wife and several neighbours at the bedside of the Goodwife of Laggan. His wife told him that the sick woman had gone out to gather peat and had returned suffering from a mysterious sickness. The hunter instantly stripped the bed coverings from the sick woman to reveal that her body was savagely torn and gashed. He related his adventures in the herdsman's cottage and the villagers promptly pulled the old woman from her bed and hanged her on the nearest tree.

Later that same night two travellers on the Badenoch road were terrified to see the bloody apparition of an old woman rushing past them hotly pursued by two gigantic coal-black dogs. Seconds later a man heavily muffled in a black coat and mounted on a black horse thundered towards them. As the mysterious rider drew level with them he shouted, 'Can she reach Dalarossie graveyard before the dogs catch her?' When the startled travellers replied in the negative the weird horseman shrieked aloud with wild laughter then disappeared into the night. A few minutes later they heard screams and the horseman reappeared but this time with the body of a woman slung across his saddle. The two enormous hounds raced beside the horse and kept leaping up and snarling at the woman's body. It was later agreed that the apparition had been that of the Goodwife of Laggan trying desperately to reach the sanctuary of the churchyard but no one attempted to even guess at the identity of the mysterious rider in black!

5 'A witches' brew'

Like the curious ingredients that furiously bubbled and boiled in the witches' legendary iron cauldrons, the contents of this particular chapter are many and varied, a motley collection of strange and unusual tales from Scottish folklore and history.

In the year 1696 a young girl by the name of Christian Shaw saw her father's maidservant, Katherine Campbell, taking a drink from the milk-churn. Christian threatened to tell her father and the maidservant, annoyed at having been found out, promptly cursed her, saying, 'May the Devil hurl your soul through hell!'

A few days later an old woman called Agnes Naismith, who had an evil reputation in Renfrewshire, asked Christian how old she was and the child answered her in a cheeky fashion.

The following night Christian had a fit and her entire body became racked with violent pains. Soon she became feverish and began to rant and rave and in her delirium she accused Katherine Campbell and Agnes Naismith of being witches. Suddenly Christian began to vomit strange substances such as small chicken bones, gravel, pebbles, candlegrease and egg-shells, together with a quantity of bent pins. Her parents were convinced that she was bewitched and the authorities were quickly informed.

The sick child was soon persuaded to implicate other villagers as being members of a local witch coven. In all 20 people were accused including 17-year-old Elizabeth Anderson, her cousin, James Lindsay, who was 14 and his 12-year-old brother, Thomas. Jean Fulton, Alexander Anderson and a noted warlock called John Reid were also named by the hysterical girl.

Five of the unfortunate twenty were burned on 10 June 1697 on the Gallow Green at Paisley. They were all burned alive. John Reid hanged himself in prison although the official report stated that he had been strangled by the Devil to prevent him from revealing too many coven secrets.

Christian Shaw later became the wife of the Reverend Miller, the minister at Kilmaurs parish. She displayed a remarkable dexterity in spinning yarn and due to her skill and a friend's knowledge of certain Dutch spinning secrets the world-famous Renfrewshire thread manufacture came into existence.

In Scotland in the year 1282 a certain John, priest of Inverkeithing, led the young and innocent maidens of his parish in a phallic

Goat of Mendes
(The Witchery
Restaurant, Edinburgh)

dance, a dance which was, according to the church authorities, to be of a decidedly obscene and disgusting nature. The dance was carried out during Easter Week. In due course penance of a suitable nature was laid upon him but strangely enough he was not really punished very severely, and was even allowed to continue as priest of the parish. Some time later the priest was murdered by an enraged parishioner who had decided in his own mind that the church authorities had been far too lenient in their sentence. It is believed that the unfortunate priest had simply remembered an ancient magical custom, one long known in the district, without actually realising its pagan sources.

Throughout the history of witchcraft there have been numerous instances of witches making an unholy pact with the Devil. In every case the pact has turned out to be somewhat one-sided and the story of William Barton illustrates this rather well.

Barton was arrested in 1655 on charges of witchcraft and after he had confessed to the various charges he told the court the following strange story. It appeared that one day while travelling from Kirkliston to Queensferry he had met a beautiful young woman. Soon the pair were on the friendliest of terms and to his delight the young woman readily agreed to meet him again. After a few more very pleasant meetings Barton discovered that the woman was, in fact, the Devil.

Barton agreed to renounce his Christian baptism and to become a follower of Satan in return for magical powers. As was usual he received the traditional Devil's mark and was given the witch name of John Baptist together with fifteen Scots pounds. The Devil also gave him a coin and told him to spend it at Queensferry but warned him not to spend the remainder of the money.

To the surprise of the assembled court Barton suddenly burst out laughing and when questioned about his strange behaviour stated that although he had confessed, he would never be executed. He went on to say that his master, the Devil, had solemnly promised him that 'No man will ever take my life!' Even on the actual day of his execution, Barton was still firmly convinced that the Devil would keep his word. When the prison guard told him that the stake had been erected and the execution fire built he still continued to laugh. Strangely enough when the official executioner entered Barton's cell he suddenly collapsed and died. The authorities, however, immediately took the rather unusual step of appointing the executioner's wife to carry out the sentence of strangulation. Barton went to his death screaming, 'The Devil has deceived me. Never let anyone else trust his promises!'

In the small village of Torryburn in the west of Fife in the year 1704, an old woman, Lillias Adie, was accused of bringing ill health to one of her neighbours, a certain Jean Nelson. Summoned before the ministers and elders of Torryburn church, poor old confused Lillias confessed that she was indeed a witch. She told the grim-faced committee of church elders that she had met the Devil in a cornfield and had accepted him as her lover and master. The terrified woman described how she and the Devil had led many others, whom she named, in a wild heathenish dance. According to Lillias a strange blue unearthly light had appeared and had followed the dancers round the cornfield. Her tales grew wilder and wilder and were eagerly accepted as proof of her dealings with the

Devil. Lillias was, according to the official records, 'burnt within the sea-mark'.

In the year 1677 there occurred a rather curious case of witchcraft in Haddington in East Lothian. It took place during a church service when several members of the congregation happened to notice a servant woman called Lizzie Mudie behaving in a somewhat strange fashion. Lizzie was seen and heard to count aloud on her fingers and when she had reached the total of fifty-nine was heard to say 'There, the turn is done.' Later that day it was discovered that Lizzie Mudie's mistress, Margaret Kirkwood had hanged herself in her own home. When it was realised that the dead woman had been 59 years of age Lizzie Mudie was immediately arrested on the suspicion of witchcraft. The traditional Devil's mark was eventually found on her body and after the usual suitable forms of persuasion had been applied she speedily confessed to her crimes.

Lizzie also implicated a number of other unfortunates, five women and a man, two of the women being well-known local midwives. One of those she accused was an old woman of 80, Marion Phin, who complained vehemently after three months in prison about the dreadful conditions and the slur to her good character and name. The council earnestly considered her petition to be released but, as was only to be expected, refused it. Orders were then given that she should be tried immediately as a witch.

If East Lothian and, in particular, the Royal Burgh of Haddington were notorious in olden days for witchcraft, so also was the tiny village of Longniddry. The village itself has now changed almost beyond recognition; modern housing estates have completely altered the character of this once quiet backwater of rural tranquillity. In 1591 a young boy called Alexander Fairlie was apparently bewitched by a certain Beigis Tod, a well-known local practitioner of witchcraft. For over two months the unfortunate youth was subject to fainting fits, stomach disorders and terrifying hallucinations. Night after night his sleep was rudely disturbed by weird visitations from a large black shaggy dog and sometimes by the shadowy shape of Beigis Tod herself.

Beigis Tod and her motley crew of weird friends were all well-known witches in the district and most of the local inhabitants were careful to give them a very wide berth. It was rumoured that they met late at night at the Deane-Fute beside a circle of ancient standing stones and there did practise their evil sorcery.

In 1594 their master, the Devil himself, paid a visit and after celebrating with strong drink, meat and song they carried out a weird ceremony of passing a cat nine times through a 'cruik', a large hook for hanging a cooking-pot above the fire. After this they set off for a neighbouring village where they christened the unfortunate cat with the name of Margaret before sacrificing it to Satan. Eventually Beigis Tod and most of her coven were arrested and taken to the Castle Hill, where they were first strangled at the stake then burned in the execution fire.

One of the most interesting characters in olden day Longniddry was the 'pyper's mother' who seems to have been a somewhat malevolent person. It seems that she paid a visit one night to a woman who lived in Dirleton, a small village not far from Longniddry and while there tried to persuade her to become a servant of Satan. Not surprisingly the startled woman refused, whereupon the entire house became 'filled with a black wind and an evil stinking mist.'

Despite the most fearful curses and dreadful imprecations the terrified woman steadfastly refused to become one of Satan's followers and eventually the 'pyper's mother' departed in a rather bad temper. Hardly had she left, however, when the Devil himself burst into the house in the shape of a large black dog. To the housewife's horror the dog suddenly transformed itself into a 'black man' who promptly assaulted the poor woman before she had a chance to defend herself. The 'pyper's mother' was arrested soon after and paid the usual grim penalty of being burned at the stake.

In addition to being heavily plagued by witchcraft, Scotland also seems, even in the early days of its history, to have had more than its fair share of strange and curious supernatural happenings. During the reign of King Caratake, for example, there were seen numerous ghostly apparitions of heavily armed horsemen fighting and killing each other. In a country district a child was apparently born with a raven's head and elsewhere the sun itself was completely covered, for a period of six months, in heavy, dark clouds. During a battle with Roman legionaries an armed man flew high above the heads of the advancing Scottish army then mysteriously vanished. In the year 697 blood rained down from the heavens and the sound of two great armies fighting could be clearly heard although there was nothing visible. According to legend a mysterious ghost also danced at a ball being held at Jedburgh during the wedding festivities of Alexander III in 1285.

On Christmas Eve in the year 1466, a certain John Cameron, Bishop of Glasgow, who had led a wicked and extremely dissolute life, was sound asleep in bed when a tremendous crash of thunder awoke him. A terrifying voice then commanded him to appear before the 'court of God' to be tried for his various crimes. The frightened clergyman shouted for his servants to attend him and then a second crash of thunder was heard. Again the voice spoke to him. Moments later came a third clap of thunder and once more the dreaded voice repeated its grim unearthly summons. The startled servants saw their master fall back heavily on his bed, utter a dreadful groan, then, with tongue hanging from his mouth, die – as though strangled by unseen hands!

During the year 1480 a ship set sail from Scotland to Flanders. Although it was the middle of summer a tremendous hurricane blew up and the ship was tossed around like a cork on the waves. The storm became so violent that the crew were convinced that they would all perish, but suddenly one of the passengers, a woman, ordered them to throw her into the raging sea.

The woman confessed that she had been haunted for several years by an incubus (an evil spirit in the shape of a man) and that if she was drowned the crew would all be saved and she would be rid of the spirit. Another of the passengers, a priest, rushed forward and began to pray for the woman's soul. In the midst of his prayers there came a tremendous explosion and a huge, black, stinking cloud burst out from the bowels of the ship. Enveloped in flames, it crashed into the sea and instantly the fierce hurricane ceased. The rest of the journey was completed without any further mishaps and the ship reached port safely.

Many years ago, in Scotland, in the county of the Earl of Mar, a young and very beautiful noblewoman puzzled her parents by her continued refusal to every offer of marriage. Then one day she confessed that she was heavy with child and when her angry and distraught parents demanded to know the name of the father she told them that a young man frequently visited her late at night and sometimes even during the day. She said that she was unable to tell them who he was or how he was able to enter the house unobserved.

The entire household kept a close watch over the next few nights and then three nights later one of the female servants caught an unknown man entering the girl's bedroom. Alerted by the servant's terrified screams the infuriated parents together with a crowd of angry friends and neighbours, all carrying lit torches, burst into the room. To their horror they saw that a foul and hideous monster lay in bed embracing the girl, who seemed completely unaware of her secret lover's terrible appearance. Amongst those present in the room was the local priest, a man well versed in the holy scriptures, who promptly began to recite part of the gospel according to St John. Uttering a ferocious and unearthly scream the evil spirit ripped off the roof of the bedchamber then flew away, leaving the bedclothes on fire as it vanished. Three days later the girl gave birth to a hideously misshapen beast which the midwife and the other women present promptly burned in a huge fire which had been built expressly for that very purpose.

A shoemaker called Robert Heckspeckle who lived in Selkirk had the habit of being at his workbench very early every morning. One particular morning a stranger entered his tiny shop wearing a long black cloak with a wide-brimmed hat pulled down over his eyes. After looking round the shop the stranger lifted a shoe from the bench and tried it on. The shoe fitted perfectly and the mysterious stranger paid in gold and told the shoemaker that he would return for the other shoe before cock-crow the following morning.

Later that day Robert Heckspeckle became suspicious of his strange customer. He remembered that the stranger's clothes had smelt extremely mouldy and he had the horrible impression that among the gold coins in the stranger's purse had been worms, beetles and a handful of earth. A rather worried shoemaker went early to bed that evening and spent the entire night tossing and turning.

The following morning, true to his word, the stranger again entered the shoemaker's shop and collected the second shoe, again paying for it with a gold coin. When the mysterious customer left the shop the worried shoemaker followed him at a discreet distance. To his amazement his weird customer entered the local graveyard, walked to a grave, jumped into it and disappeared.

The shoemaker immediately hurried back to the village, collected several neighbours then returned to the graveyard. The villagers dug up the grave and when they opened the mouldering

Frontispiece of *Discovery of Witches*, 1644

coffin they found that the corpse inside was wearing the new shoes. The shoemaker immediately reclaimed the shoes then hurried back to his shop.

Early the next morning the shoemaker's wife heard her husband whistling and banging away in his workshop. Suddenly she heard her husband scream, there was a terrible crash then complete silence. Rushing into the room the startled housewife found it completely empty, but above the shoemaker's bench there lingered a faint but unmistakable smell of sulphur and on the floor lay a small heap of mouldering earth. When the stranger's grave was again reopened, the horrified villagers found the corpse once more wearing its new shoes, while clutched tightly in its right hand was the shoemaker's tassled nightcap. The unfortunate shoemaker was never seen again, at least, not by mere mortal eyes!

A strange case of haunting took place in North Berwick, a small seaside town in East Lothian, during the latter part of the eighteenth century. It happened when a certain weaver's wife died giving birth to their fourth child; the unfortunate woman, who had been extremely beautiful, was seized with tremendous convulsions and became terribly disfigured. The weaver's neighbours were all of the opinion that the woman had been carried away by elves, who had left a ghastly corpse in her place. After a year of mourning the weaver decided that, with a young family to look after, he should remarry. In due course the banns were called and preparations for the wedding were made.

One night before the wedding, however, the weaver awoke at the 'witching hour' of midnight to find his dead wife standing at the foot of the bed. Dressed in white, the apparition gazed down at him then told him that she was not dead but was a prisoner in Elfland. The weaver was told that on a certain day of the following week he was to gather together all the respectable housewives of North Berwick. Led by the local minister they were to walk to the cemetery and there they were to open the grave and dig up the coffin. The terrified weaver was then instructed that certain prayers were to be said and once this had been done the corpse would leap from the coffin and run swiftly round the church. The local blacksmith, who was also the fastest runner in the parish, was to pursue her, catch hold of her and then she would resume her mortal form.

When he rose next morning the weaver spent all day worrying about his strange visitation. Eventually he decided to ignore what he had been told, certain that it had only been a dream. That same night, however, his dead wife visited him again and repeated her words of the previous night. On the third night the apparition appeared once more but this time she warned him that if he failed to carry out the instructions he had been given it would be the last time he would ever see or speak to her.

The following day the terrified man went to see his local minister, one Matthew Reid, and told him of his strange nightly visits. The clergyman, who seems to have been a very understanding and extremely compassionate person, listened sympathetically to the strange and incredible tale. He neither attempted to argue with the weaver nor to deny the truth of his story but instead he gently explained that he had no authority to open graves or to exhume the dead. 'My best advice' said the minister, 'is to get married as quickly as possible. Today or tomorrow if you can. I will agree to dispensing with the calling of the rest of the banns. Rest assured that your late wife, God bless her, sleeps in peace.' The weaver took the minister's wise advice and was never again troubled by ghostly apparitions or strange nightly visitations.

An extremely strange series of weird supernatural happenings took place in Glenluce in Galloway about the turn of the seventeenth century. The terrifying happenings began when Alexander Agnew, a beggar, was refused alms by a weaver called Gilbert Campbell. Agnew promptly cursed the entire family and, not long afterwards, Gilbert's wife, Jennifer, began to hear curious shrill whistling sounds.

However, the real trouble did not begin until late November, when showers of stones literally bombarded the walls and roof of Campbell's house. Day after day the invisible stone-thrower carried out his malicious pranks and hundreds of stones even cascaded down the chimney. Curiously enough none of the family was ever hurt by any of the thrown stones.

Eventually Campbell, almost driven frantic with worry, confided in his local minister and from that moment on his troubles increased. The threads on his working looms were cut as though by invisible scissors and then even the very clothes the family were wearing were slashed and ripped to shreds. Their bedclothes were pulled from their beds while they slept and drawers and cupboard doors flew open and the contents were hurled around the house. Household utensils mysteriously vanished and bales of cloth were slashed and torn until the poor distraught weaver was eventually forced to give up his trade.

Some of his neighbours who were convinced that the source of his strange troubles originated from one of his family advised him to send his children away. Campbell took their advice and things actually quietened down for a few days but then the minister persuaded him to bring his family back to the house. When Thomas, one of his sons who had been sent farther afield, returned to the family home, all Hell literally broke out. This time the invisible prankster took to lighting fires in different parts of the house and Campbell and his neighbours were soon kept busy putting out innumerable small fires.

Campbell then persuaded the local minister to keep his son Thomas for a few days, hoping that this might bring an end to his strange troubles. The troubles only increased, however, and night after night the members of his family suffered from mysterious blows and painful pricking with invisible pins. Someone or something kept knocking holes in the walls and roof and Campbell was almost driven mad with worry. Eventually he sent for his son Thomas to come back to the house.

Thomas told his father that a voice had forbidden him to enter his own home or any other place where the trade of weaving was being carried on. Ignoring the ominous warning, however, Thomas entered his father's house but was so severely beaten and bruised by an invisible attacker that he was soon forced to return to the minister's house.

The supernatural happenings went on for several months and from a study of the official records it appears logical to assume that these were due to a poltergeistic manifestation.

On a number of occasions a spirit voice held a lengthy conversation with the Campbell family. The voice stated that it was an evil spirit from the very depths of Hell and that Satan himself was its father. On one occasion a naked arm and hand appeared and began beating furiously on the floor. Soon the entire house began to shake and the voice started shouting, 'Come up, father, come up, father!' The minister himself witnessed the various manifestations and also heard the voice utter a number of predictions for the future. Strangely enough all of these predictions were duly fulfilled. The spirit even appeared to display a certain sly humour and on one occasion asked Campbell's daughter, Janet, if she would give him her belt. When the girl asked what the spirit needed it for she was told, 'I need it to fasten my loose bones together!'

A number of ministers gathered at Campbell's house and attempted to carry out a ceremony of exorcism but to no avail. Campbell's wife had the unpleasant experience of having oatmeal snatched from her hands when she was making porridge early one morning. When the angry housewife yelled at the spirit to return her oatmeal the demon prankster promptly obliged by hurling it back at her. For over two years the unfortunate Campbell family were terrorised by the poltergeist then suddenly, as mysteriously as it had appeared, the poltergeist vanished.

Alexander Agnew was later hanged in Dumfries for being in league with the Devil and for declaring in public, 'There was no God but salt, meal and water!'

One of the strangest and, at the same time, exceptionally well-documented cases of supernatural happenings took place in 1695 in Rerrick, Kircudbright. Andrew Mackie, a respected and God-fearing man, owned a fairly large farm known as 'Ring-Croft of Stocking'. One night in February 1695, he found several of his farm animals wandering loose around his outhouses. On the following night Mackie made sure that all of his animals were securely locked up. In the morning he again found most of them wandering about the farm. That night the family found a basket of smouldering peat in the centre of their living-room floor.

During the month of March stones were hurled at the house but no human hand was ever visible. Frequently while the family were inside their house showers of stones crashed down on them. Curiously enough no one was ever bruised or injured because the stones always struck them very lightly.

One evening Mackie's young children came into the house and saw, sitting by the fire, what looked like a body wrapped in a blanket. Recovering from their fright the children investigated and discovered a four-legged stool with a blanket draped over it. As the days went on the supernatural happenings grew worse; household utensils vanished and were found, days later, in different parts of the house.

The mysterious stone-throwing became more and more frequent until eventually the bewildered Mackie called in the local minister, the Reverend Alexander Telfair. Telfair led the family in

prayer and called on the evil spirit or spirits to depart and leave the family in peace and curiously enough during the ceremony the stone-throwing ceased. Hardly had the minister left the house, however, when the stone-throwing recommenced and this time people were seriously hurt when the stones struck them.

The Reverend Telfair bravely insisted on spending the night under Mackie's roof where, despite his prayers and fervent exhortation, he was not only struck several times by large stones but was also continually beaten by an invisible stick. Terrified onlookers could actually hear the sound of heavy blows and then strange rappings were heard all over the house. During his prayers the minister felt something pressing against him and saw a small white hand and arm – but the arm disappeared at the elbow! Some of the family and several neighbours saw a young, red-faced man with yellow hair peering at them through a window.

As the days passed the stone-throwing increased and various people were also viciously attacked by some invisible being armed with sharp claw-like nails.

The Reverend Telfair made numerous inquiries concerning Ring-Croft and its previous occupiers and a number of very strange facts soon emerged. He discovered that, at one time, there had been various rumours circulating around the parish, saying that Andrew Mackie, a mason by trade, had, when he took the Mason-word, promised his first child to the Devil. To Telfair's credit he immediately defended Mackie, stating that he was a devout and upright man and that the rumours were nothing more than base slanderous statements.

It was also said that a woman who enjoyed an evil reputation had left some clothes in the house but had died before getting them back. Some of the villagers said that Mackie had kept the clothes although he had insisted that he had returned them to the woman's friends.

Telfair also found out that a previous occupier, a man called MacKnaught, had suffered from a variety of misfortunes while living in the house. Eventually MacKnaught sent his son to visit a local witch to see whether she could give him some explanation for his run of ill luck. According to the local legend his son met some soldiers while returning home and went abroad with them without making any attempt to let his father know the witch's answer.

Many years later another villager called John Redick met the

Examples of various tarot cards (author's collection)

young man in Flanders and the youth asked him if, on his return home, he would seek out his father or whoever now lived in the house. MacKnaught's son went on to say that the witch had told him that buried under the threshold of the front door was a tooth and that unless this tooth was burned no one living in the house would ever prosper. When Redick eventually returned to his village he discovered that old MacKnaught had died and that his wife had left the house, which now stood empty. As time went on Redick forgot about the affair and it was only when the strange happenings took place during Mackie's occupancy of the house that he remembered his conversation with MacKnaught's son.

The Reverend Telfair also found out that between MacKnaught and Mackie's ownership of the house it had belonged to a certain Thomas Telfair, who had found the tooth and had thrown it into the fire, where it had apparently burnt like a wax candle.

As the months passed the stone-throwing continued and various members of the family together with some of their neighbours saw the figure of a young boy wearing a bonnet and grey clothing moving around the farm. Some of Mackie's neighbours who visited him found themselves hurled violently to the ground by a powerful but unseen force, which then proceeded to drag them furiously around the house. Inside the house itself bedclothes were dragged from the beds and furniture and household utensils could be seen moving around the various rooms as though some invisible person was carrying them. On numerous occasions whistling sounds were heard and strange noises became quite commonplace.

Various members of the clergy came to visit Mackie and themselves witnessed many of the strange supernatural happenings. It seems that the weird disturbances always seemed to increase during prayer-meetings and frequently burning peat was thrown through the windows. Barns were set on fire and the stone-throwing increased to such a pitch that, at times, it resembled a shower of hailstones.

One night Mackie's wife found a loose flagstone at the entrance to the house and when she lifted it up she made rather a gruesome discovery. Beneath the loose stone lay several curious items – seven small bones together with bloody particles of flesh wrapped in a piece of old tattered paper. To her horror Mackie's wife realised that the bloodstains on the paper were fresh and bright. After this discovery the supernatural happenings increased in ferocity and enormous fireballs now began to be hurled around the house while huge red-hot stones crashed through the roof. One of the visiting clergy held a prayer-meeting then left the house carrying the parcel of bones and flesh.

For a while Mackie and his terrified family were left in peace, then the forces of evil suddenly redoubled their malignant efforts. Heavy farm implements levitated in front of startled onlookers and were hurled in various different directions.

One evening Mackie's eldest son, John Mackie, came home from visiting friends in the village and during his return was enveloped in a strange bright flame which accompanied him all the way.

A few days later Andrew Mackie found a letter lying on his doorstep. The letter was written and sealed in blood and on the back of the letter were written the following words: 'Three years tho shall have to repent net it well.'

Shortly after this episode everyone living in the village was ordered to attend a special meeting in the local village hall. Once everyone had been assembled the local magistrate ordered them to file past the parcel of bones and flesh discovered by Mackie's wife. According to an ancient superstition it was believed that if a murder had been carried out, the corpse, or parts of it, would flow with fresh blood should the murderer lay hands upon it. Each person was ordered to touch the grisly parcel but, needless to say, nothing strange took place.

From February 1695 until April, Mackie and his long-suffering family were continually tormented by different supernatural occurrences. On 28 April the farmhouse was set on fire no less than seven times – each time the family quenched one fire, another broke out in a separate part of the building. On one occasion the entire gable-end of the house collapsed and the family fled in terror as heavy stones crashed around them. Towards the end of April various witnesses saw a weird black object in the corner of the barn, an object that rapidly increased in size then changed suddenly into a strange black cloud which slowly and dramatically vanished into the ground.

The terrifying sequence of bizarre and inexplicable happenings ceased after 1 May 1695 and from that day to this there has never been a satisfactory explanation of the curious Rerrick haunting.

Another curious case of strange supernatural happenings involving a poltergeist is said to have taken place in Galashiels, where a young girl, Margaret Wilson, became the unwilling victim. Each night when the family were at supper loud rappings could be heard coming from beneath her chair. When Margaret went to bed strange knockings seemed to come from beneath the bed but a search revealed nothing unusual.

Eventually the local minister, the Reverend Wilkie, was called in to investigate and to hold the usual prayer-meeting in an attempt to exorcise the unruly spirit. During one of his visits Margaret fell into a deep sleep and then suddenly her unconscious body rose slowly into the air. Even when a number of strong men attempted to hold her down she still continued to rise above the bed. It was also discovered that if her feet were held then the upper part of her body continued to move up and down. Weird scratching noises came from the feather-bed and a curious rasping sound could be heard coming from the region of her heart. When the unfortunate girl finally awoke she stated that the Devil himself had spoken to her.

The Reverend Wilkie, who seems to have been a remarkably astute man, took the girl's uncle into the garden and questioned him closely on his behaviour towards her. The uncle angrily denied ever having done anything to offend God or in any way annoyed his young niece. The minister mentioned one thing in particular but again the girl's uncle denied having been responsible. Shortly afterwards the 13-year-old girl was sent to Edinburgh and then became a servant with a family in Leith. Curiously enough the supernatural happenings ceased as soon as she left her uncle's house.

A story from the seventeenth century shows how poltergeism might be linked with witchcraft. The local minister of Peaston in the parish of Ormiston had a servant, Isobel Heriot, who was small, slim and with a dark complexion. She had, for a servant woman in those days, a somewhat over-confident and rather sarcastic manner and eventually the minister took a strong dislike to her and dismissed her from his service. Isobel Heriot fell ill during the winter months of 1680 from some strange unknown form of sickness. Her face turned black and her body seemed to slowly wither and waste away then after a few days she died.

She had only been buried a few hours when the rumours began to spread, rumours that her apparition, dressed in a shroud, had been seen walking from the chapel to the minister's house. Several nights later showers of stones crashed against the walls of the manse and whenever the minister appeared he was immediately pelted with rocks although there did not appear to be anyone else in the vicinity. One or two other people in the parish were also plagued by the mysterious stone-thrower and then one night the minister's stable-boy was attacked by some invisible creature which seized hold of his legs. Morning after morning the unfortunate minister also discovered his horse lathered in sweat as though it had been ridden hard during the night.

In the days that followed the ghostly attacks became worse: household objects were hurled through the air, burning coals were discovered under the beds and in linen-cupboards and the stone-throwing increased until the minister was almost driven mad with fear and worry.

A month later Isobel Heriot's ghost was seen, dressed in a shroud and with blackened face, walking in the minister's garden. As the apparition walked it was heard to mutter, 'A stane, a stane', and was seen to gather stones which it laid in a pile at the bottom of the garden. A woman, returning home late one evening, met the ghost and had the courage to ask it why it had returned to haunt and persecute the minister. In deep, sombre tones the apparition replied: 'The reason for my return is that I wronged my master when I served him. I stole his gold and hid it underneath the hearthstone in the kitchen. Later I sold it in the Canongate, Edinburgh!'

The ghost then went on to say that one night before she fell ill she had been returning from Edinburgh when her horse had stumbled and to her horror the Devil himself had risen from the ground in front of her. Satan had ordered her to destroy the minister and had warned her that should she fail him he would cast her into a bottomless pit.

That was the last time Isobel Heriot's ghost appeared and after that the minister and his parishioners were left in peace. Although Isobel Heriot had never been accused during her lifetime of being a witch, tales of sorcery, witchcraft and Devil worship swiftly circulated after her death.

6 The fairy folk

Closely associated with the numerous legends of witchcraft are, of course, tales of the fairy folk, and this is especially true of Scotland. Witchcraft was, of course, a pagan religion, and its followers had the 'magical' power to heal both humans and animals. They were also believed to be able to make land, animals and even humans fertile by the use of certain curious incantations. With the coming of the Romans and also Christianity, the followers of the 'Old Religion' (the 'Craft') were eventually forced to flee to the remotest areas of the country in order to avoid persecution. Here, in time, they became known as the 'wee people', the 'fairy folk' and humans tended to regard both them and their strange powers with awe and dread. (We are, of course, describing witches of an extremely early age, before the eleventh century.)

Various authorities, including Professor Margaret Murray, firmly believed that these 'wee folk' really existed and were, in fact, early inhabitants of Scotland. There is evidence that they may actually have been a race of pygmies – short, broad-shouldered, extremely stocky people, who possessed certain semi-magical powers. It may well be true that these 'fairy folk' did steal human babies, in order to improve the physique and blood strain of their own pygmy stock. This would also explain the strange disappearances of human adults, both males and females, kidnapped for the sole purpose of inter-breeding.

According to history – or perhaps legend – Ian, the fourth chief of the Clan MacLeod, had a fairy wife, who, according to one version of the story, helped him acquire a magical banner. He and his fairy wife lived for some time in Fairyland but eventually the chief wished to return to his human world. Amidst sorrowful tears his wife presented him with a certain banner. She told him that this magical flag could be waved three times, and only three times, whenever the Clan MacLeod was in mortal danger. The banner was waved on two occasions when the Clan McLeod was in deadly peril and each time its magical powers proved to be highly success-ful. The tattered and extremely fragile remnants of the legendary Fairy Flag of Dunvegan still exist, although the actual legend itself dates as far back as the year 1380.

Although small in stature the fairy folk proved to be extremely formidable opponents in battle, even when opposed by human beings several times their size. Their incredible knowledge of herbs, drugs and also poisons was put to good use in the many and ferocious battles they had with various enemies.

The legendary and deadly 'elf-arrows' had their sharp tips anointed with deadly poisons, for which there was at that time no known or effective antidote.

The use of the fabled 'elf-arrows' was the means by which the fairy folk won many hard-fought battles despite apparently overwhelming odds. In the year 1598 for example, on the Island of Islay, a furious battle was about to break out between two famous clans, the Clan MacDonalds and the Clan Macleans. The Mac-Donalds had taken the very sensible precaution of engaging the valuable services of a certain 'Black Elf' – a famous fairy archer. Just as the battle was about to commence, 'Black Elf' took careful aim and then, with deadly accuracy, shot one arrow, which killed the opposing leader instantly – an arrow tipped with a deadly and extremely virulent poison. That was the end of the battle!

Near Inverness stands the fairy hill called Tomnahurich. The famous Brahan Seer predicted that it would one day be kept under lock and key and that the fairies would be kept secure within, and his strange prophecy came true a century later when Tomnahurich was turned into a Christian cemetery with a fence built around it and a gate which was locked each night at sunset. Towering over 220 ft above sea-level, with heavy undergrowth covering the land round about, Tomnahurich still retains a somewhat wild and untamed appearance. According to legend, it was on this spot that the famous Thomas the Rhymer was chosen by the Fairy Queen as her lover (the story is told below) and another charming story relates how a certain Donald the Fiddler was inveigled into the fairy hill.

Donald, who was notoriously lazy, much preferred fiddling to carrying out his trade as a tanner. One evening, after a fairly heavy bout of drinking, he fell asleep near the fairy hill, and woke suddenly to find an old man wearing a heavy velvet cloak trimmed with fur and tied with a crimson sash bending over him. Noticing his fiddle, the old man invited Donald to go with him to a party to make music there. As soon as Donald accepted the invitation he found himself inside a magnificent mansion and was led to a beautiful ballroom where he played his fiddle for hours. The tables were loaded with an array of fantastic food and drink, and the rest of the musicians were playing heavenly music. Donald's only problem was that the guests danced and danced without ever stopping to rest. Completely exhausted and beginning to believe that the guests must be almost super-human, Donald cried out in exasperation, 'Holy St Mary, help me. What shall I do?'

Instantly, in the twinkling of an eye, everything vanished and Donald found himself lying shivering near the river-bank beside his home. Standing up, Donald walked towards the town but it seemed to be much larger than when he last remembered it, and less familiar. With a sudden flash of inspiration Donald realised that instead of spending a single night in the enchanted mansion he had actually been there for a hundred years. Slowly he made his way towards a nearby chapel, St Mary's, where his antiquated clothing made the worshippers laugh. Their laughter soon ceased when, at the first words of the service, Donald collapsed in a heap of decaying flesh and bones. The worshippers very quickly buried him.

One of the most famous tales of a mere mortal being taken as a lover by one of the fairy folk, in this case none other than the Fairy Queen herself, is the charming legend of Thomas the Rhymer. As mentioned earlier in this chapter, it was believed by some authorities that this meeting took place at the famous fairy hill known as Tomnahurich. However, according to other authorities, the meeting actually took place at the Eildon Hills near Melrose and I think that this is probably more accurate. Thomas was born at Ercel-doune (Earlston, Berwick) in Lauderdale during the reign of Alexander III of Scotland (thirteenth century) and was widely renowned as a poet. According to the legend, Thomas was lying one day beside a river-bank when a beautiful woman suddenly appeared before him. She was mounted on a magnificent white horse whose mane was richly decorated with 39 silver bells (three times 13, the number of three witch covens). Her saddle was made of pure ivory and beautifully inlaid with gold filigree work. In one hand she held a golden bow, and a quiver of arrows hung at her golden belt. Three greyhounds were held on a golden leash and three more hounds followed close behind.

Thomas instantly fell deeply in love with this beautiful vision and declared his intention to pay his fair visitor all due homage. The Fairy Queen, for it was none other, told him that he must first become her slave and do her bidding. Then to Thomas's horror she suddenly changed her appearance and turned into a hideous old hag. One side of her body was wasted and diseased, one of her eyes hung down and her complexion was of a leaden hue. Yet horrific though her appearance was, Thomas could not help but follow her. He found himself entering a dark cave and for three days he went after his ghastly guide. Sometimes he found himself wading through rivers of blood and he could hear the distant sounds of an ocean. Suddenly they emerged into bright sunlight and Thomas found himself in a beautiful orchard. Ravenous for want of food Thomas reached out to pluck an apple. Before he could eat it, however, his strange guide warned him that the fruit was of the same type as that which had once caused the downfall of the human race. Thomas then discovered that as soon as his guide had entered the orchard she had recovered her former beauty; in fact, she was now even more beautiful than before.

The Fairy Queen commanded Thomas to lay his head upon her knee whilst she explained certain things to him: 'The right-hand path' she said ,'leads the blessed to Paradise. That well worn path yonder takes souls to the place of everlasting punishment. That third path leads to a region where souls may be released through constant prayer. But the fourth road leads to our destination. It is the road to Elfland. The lord of yonder castle is the King of Fairyland and I am his queen. He must never know that you are to be my secret lover. From now on you must never utter a single word, else you will instantly be transported to the land of mortals and will see me no more!'

Once she was completely sure that Thomas fully understood her instructions the Fairy Queen led him towards the castle. Entering by the kitchen they found themselves in the midst of tremendous festive preparations. Over 30 carcasses of deer were being carved up by numerous cooks. Massive haunches of venison were being prepared and enormous cooking pots were being stirred by various kitchen servants. Turkeys, chickens and all manner of different fowl were being basted over huge open fires. Enormous meat pies and succulent pastries were being stacked high on the already overloaded and groaning tables. The smell of the food made Thomas, who by now was starving, feel faint but his guide led him on until they reached the royal hall.

The King of the Fairies welcomed both his queen and her companion without apparently suspecting their illicit liaison. Knights and their ladies were dancing on the floor of the hall and Thomas,

all fatigue forgotten, joined in the revelry. After what seemed to him to be only a few hours Thomas was approached by the Fairy Queen. When told that it was now time for him to return to his own world Thomas argued that he had only been dancing for a very short time. 'How long' answered the queen 'do you think you have been here?' 'My lady,' answered Thomas 'no more than seven short days.' 'My love,' said the queen 'you have been here full seven years and it is now time you were gone. Know you that tomorrow the very fiend of Hell himself will come to this place and demand your soul. This I will not have, so thee must go now!'

To his astonishment the next instant Thomas found himself lying once more on the river bank. Beside him stood his fairy lover but before she took her final farewell the Fairy Queen bestowed upon him the rare gift of 'the tongue which could not lie'! From that day onwards Thomas the Rhymer possessed the power of prophecy and all of his utterances came true.

For a number of years Thomas lived in his home town enjoying the reputation brought to him by his fairy gift. Then one day whilst he was entertaining the Earl of March a hart and a hind entered the village. Immediately he learned of the appearance of these normally shy animals the prophet declared that he was once more being summoned to go to Elfland. Thomas followed the two animals into the forest and vanished from mortal sight. After that he was only seen rarely, by certain human beings who conversed with him briefly on matters magical. According to legend Thomas has, on certain occasions, been prevailed upon to make an appearance when Scotland has been faced with some dire crisis.

Once a horse-vendor sold a black horse to a man of old and venerable appearance. He was told that if he brought the horse at midnight to a certain hillock upon the Eildon Hills called the Lucken-hare he would receive his money. The horse-dealer duly went to the meeting-place at the appointed hour and was paid in ancient golden coins. The aged man then invited the dealer to view his residence and at once an opening appeared in the hillside. To his astonishment the dealer found himself looking at rows of stables. In each stable stood a motionless horse and at the feet of each horse lay a warrior armed and dressed in full armour. The wizard, for such the old man was, then told the horse-dealer that all these armed men would awaken at the Battle of Sheriffmoor. At the far end of the cavern hung a sword and a horn and the dealer was told that these could be used to break the spell. Thoroughly confused, and also more than a little terrified, he attempted to blow the horn. Immediately the horses came alive and furiously stamped their hooves until the very stalls shook and trembled. At the same instant the sleeping warriors rose and pounded their swords upon their shields. A tremendous voice roared through the underground chamber and pronounced the immortal words:

Woe to the coward that ever he was born,
That did not draw the sword before he blew the horn!

A furious whirlwind blew the unfortunate horse-dealer from the cavern and he was never again able to find the secret doorway.

One of the most famous cases of an attempt by the fairy folk to steal a human child occurred many years ago in the area of Kircudbright. In a small cottage near Auchneight lived a herd and his wife who were in the service of Sir Godfrey M'Culloch. The herd's wife had just given birth to a small child when the herd received an urgent summons to attend his master. There were so many important domestic matters to attend to that it was quite late in the day before the servant was able to set out on his long journey.

On the way, the herd was forced to pass a certain spot well known for being haunted by the 'wee folk'. To make matters even worse it was Hallowe'en, a time of ghosts and hob-goblins. To his horror, as he neared the infamous spot he noticed a faint light approaching him. As he watched, it began to take on the form of a coach, drawn by six horses and lit by several blue lamps. The coach was packed with tiny elfish figures and a weird bodyguard galloped furiously behind it. A tiny blue torch, the signal of death, was burning by the side of the roadway. The terrified man was only too well aware that his young wife and his new-born child were alone in their cottage.

At midnight his wife heard the jingling of horse bridles and the stamping of horses' hooves. She could hear the excited babble of many voices and the creaking of carriage wheels. Frightened out of her wits she clasped her baby tightly in her arms and waited in sheer terror to see what was going to happen. The cottage door suddenly flew open and the entire room was lit by an unearthly blue light. All at once the kitchen was filled with dozens of tiny people dressed in fairy green.

Through the open door there entered a tall, imposing figure, richly dressed and with an imperious manner. The figure waved its hand and instantly the room fell silent. Looking at the terrified woman the stranger said, 'Tonight is All-Hallows Eve. My people and I have come for your child – and, in the Devil's name, we will have him!' 'God forbid!' the woman screamed out in agony, and instantly there was total darkness and complete silence in the room. Not unnaturally the woman fainted but when she eventually recovered her senses she found to her delight that her newborn child was sleeping soundly in his bed. Some little time later the owner of a nearby farm saw a group of tiny horsemen and a strange unearthly coach thunder past his front door.

Sir Godfrey M'Culloch himself was the subject of a curious case of 'brownie' magic. According to legend, as a young man he was once sitting looking out of a window of his house whilst workmen were building a new sewer from it to the White Loch just below, when to his surprise a little old man with snowy white hair and beard suddenly appeared beside him. The stranger was wearing a green, curiously cut costume, and seemed to be in a state of furious anger. The young man asked, in the politest of manners, how he could best serve him. To his astonishment his strange visitor replied, 'Sir, I am the King of the Brownies. For years my palace has been inside the very mound your scoundrels are, at this moment, ripping apart in order to build a sewer.'

Without any hesitation Sir Godfrey immediately ordered his workmen to cease their labours and then asked his visitor which direction he would like the new sewer to take. The pacified brownie indicated his wishes then stated that if ever Sir Godfrey M'Culloch required his magical assistance he would always be ready to help him.

Some time later the young man, having squandered his inheritance, was forced to move to a smaller house at Cardoness. A neighbour, one William Gordon, stole some of M'Culloch's cattle which had strayed on to his own land and M'Culloch immediately led a party of friends to retrieve the stolen animals. During the ensuing argument Godfrey M'Culloch shot his neighbour, breaking the unfortunate man's thigh-bone, as a result of which Gordon died some few hours later. Sir Godfrey was forced to flee and disappeared for several years. Eventually he returned to Edinburgh and whilst attending a religious service was recognised by a man in the church congregation. He was arrested, tried and condemned to death.

On the day of his execution a tremendous crowd of excited spectators gathered at the Castle Hill to witness the macabre scene. To their astonishment they saw a tiny old man with white beard and hair, dressed in an ancient suit of green and mounted on a huge white horse. The strange apparition appeared to come from the Castle Rock itself, cross the loch and ride straight up to the execution cart.

Without a second's hesitation the condemned man swung himself onto the horse behind the old man. The horse with its strange rider immediately recrossed the loch and mounted the Castle Rock then vanished. When the terrified and startled crowd looked back they saw what seemed to be Sir Godfrey M'Culloch still standing in the cart beside the executioner and the minister. Even when his head rolled upon the ground leaving a bleeding corpse behind, it was loudly rumoured throughout Edinburgh that 'It was not him himself; it was just a kind of glamour [bewitchment].' The King of the Brownies had repaid his debt.

There has always been a very strong connection between witches and fairies in Scottish witchcraft. The 'wee folk' often met and feasted with witches at the infamous Witches' Sabbats, and human beings might be given the power of the 'second sight' or the ability to cast spells as a result of their meeting with one of the fairy people.

Perhaps one of the best examples is the case of Bessie Dunlop, who was accused of being a witch and of practising the evil and black arts of sorcery. The year was 1576 and this celebrated trial took place in Lyne, in the Barony of Dalry, Ayrshire.

Bessie or Elizabeth Dunlop was asked by the court what strange powers she used to prophesy illness and how she was able to discover lost or stolen property. Bessie replied that she had no such power but if someone came to her seeking help in such matters then she asked help from a certain Thome Reid who immediately supplied her with the necessary answer. There was, it seemed, nothing strange about her answer except for one thing – Thome Reid had died in 1547 at the Battle of Pinkie. The startled judges immediately demanded that she tell them how and where she had first met the apparition of Thome Reid and Bessie, who seemed to possess an extremely vivid imagination, told the following strange tale.

She had, it seems, been driving her cows to pasture and as she walked she had been weeping bitterly because her husband and child were sick, she herself felt unwell, and some of the farm animals were dead. At that moment Thome Reid appeared in front of her and in a most courteous and kind manner asked why she was weeping. Under the impression that she was talking to another human being Bessie told him about her various family troubles. 'Bessie,' answered the apparition, 'you have displeased God and you must make amends. Thy child shall die before you return home, two sheep will perish but your husband will recover and gain his strength.' To Bessie's astonishment the figure suddenly disappeared through a narrow hole in a stone wall, a hole too small to allow a human being to pass through.

The next time she met the mysterious stranger was at the Thorn of Dawmstarnik and he offered her untold riches if she would but deny Christendom and renounce her baptism. Bessie refused but said that she would be willing to follow his advice in smaller matters. On this occasion Thome Reid disappeared, obviously in a somewhat bad mood at her refusal to do his bidding.

A few days later he appeared to her in her own house in front of her husband and several neighbours, all of whom, however, were unaware of his presence. Bessie followed the apparition into the courtyard outside and there saw eight women and four men. (Not surprisingly this group plus Thome Reid make the traditional witch coven, that is, 13.) The assembled group greeted her in a very friendly manner and asked her if she would go with them. Bessie, who had been warned by Reid not to speak, ignored the invitation whereupon the entire company vanished in a howling wind. Thome Reid explained to Bessie that the men and women were all fairies who dwelt in the Court of Elfland and if she wished she could become one of them. Again the request was refused and once more the apparition vanished in an obvious ill humour.

Despite her repeated refusals to join the unholy crew Bessie continued to receive frequent visits from her ghostly counsellor. Whenever she was consulted about human or animal ailments or the recovery of lost or stolen property she was able, with the help of Thome Reid, to give the correct answer. Bessie also received several different types of healing ointments and was taught how to predict the recovery or death of the patient by observing the effect of the particular ointment she used. Her normal fee for help in such cases was a peck of meal and some cheese.

Curiously enough there were certain illnesses she was unable to cure; for example, Lady Kilbowie was unable to have her crooked leg straightened. The reason given by Thome Reid was that the marrow of the bone was perished and the circulation of the blood so poor that the patient's leg would never heal. A diagnosis that showed remarkable common sense, at least, and a degree of medical knowledge.

Questioned closely by her judges, Bessie Dunlop said that she had never known Thome Reid when he was alive but she knew that before his death he had been an officer to the Laird of Blair and that his son had succeeded to his office. She stated that frequently he sent her on errands to his relatives and on these occasions she had asked them to right various wrongs committed by Reid while he was alive. Bessie informed the court that Reid had always given her certain confidential information so that his relatives and friends would know that it was he who had sent her.

Surprisingly she also told the court that she had often seen Reid in various public places, in the churchyard at Dalry and often on the streets in Edinburgh. On these occasions, however, she said that she had never spoken to him as he had warned her never to approach him without his prior permission.

When asked why this particular apparition should have singled her out for his attention Bessie replied that while she had been in childbirth a stout woman had entered her cottage demanding a drink. The woman had told Bessie that her child would die but that her husband who was ill would recover in due course. Thome Reid had later explained that the stout woman was none other than the Queen of Fairies and that she had commanded him to look after Bessie and try to persuade her to visit Fairyland.

Once when she was tethering her horse at the side of Restalrig Loch she heard a tremendous rushing sound as though a large group of riders were thundering past and she had the impression that the invisible riders rode straight into the waters of the loch with a hideous rumbling noise. According to Thome Reid this was the fairy folk returning from one of their frequent visits to Earth.

Unfortunately even Thome Reid, with all of his reputed magical powers, was unable to influence the decision of the court and although Bessie's witchcraft was more beneficial than evil the verdict of the court was 'convict and burn' – and the verdict was

Witch being anointed for the Sabbat

eventually carried out.

Another curious legend in which the fairy world combines with the power of witchcraft concerns Alison Pearson of Byrehill. Alison was tried on 28 May 1588 and the charge was that she had invoked the spirits of the Devil. Like Bessie Dunlop, Alison Pearson had her own familiar in the court of Elfland and in her case this was her cousin, William Sympson.

According to Alison her cousin had been taken away by a man of Egypt (a gypsy), who took him to Egypt, where he remained for 12 years. During this time his father died as a result of opening a priest's book and reading the forbidden contents.

Alison told the assembled court that one day when she was passing through Grange Muir she fell to the ground in a strange fit of sickness and that, as she lay on the ground, a green man appeared in front of her. She said that the green man had told her that he would do her good if she would only be faithful to him. Alison commanded him in the name of God that he should tell her if he came for the good of her soul whereupon her strange visitor promptly vanished.

Hardly had Alison risen to her feet, however, when he suddenly reappeared but this time he was accompanied by a large number of men and women. Alison then told the court that, much against her will, she had been forced to go with the men and women, who were dancing and singing to the sound of pipes and fiddles. Pressed by the court for further details she stated that goblets of wine and dishes heaped with rare and costly delicacies were freely handed round.

Alison also went on to say that later when she attempted to relate her strange tale to members of her family she received a violent blow from an unseen assailant, a blow that took away all feeling in her left side and which left an ugly blemish on her skin.

She told the hushed court that she frequently saw many of these fairy people and witnessed their diabolical preparation of magical salves and ointments. Sometimes, she said, the fairy folk appeared to her in such fearful forms that her dreams were haunted for many nights afterwards.

Alison further confessed that her cousin, William Sympson, lived with the fairies and that he always warned her when they were coming. Sympson, she said, also taught her various spells and incantations and told her that whenever a whirlwind blew she could be certain that the fairies were present.

Not only peasants and uneducated fellow villagers sought Alison Pearson's magical aids to cure them of sickness, so also did many of the more enlightened and wealthier classes. The celebrated Patrick Adamson, an accomplished scholar who was also Archbishop of St Andrews, sought her help and eagerly swallowed her magic potions. According to legend his illness was magically transferred to a white palfrey which thereupon died as a result.

Unfortunately William Sympson was, like Thome Reid, totally unable to give his follower any help so far as the court's decision was concerned. Again the records bear the brief and tragic inscription, *convicta et combusta* – convicted and burned!

7 Witch-prickers

Many innocent men, women and even children were convicted solely on the somewhat dubious evidence of 'witch-prickers', professional witch-finders who were employed throughout Scotland to discover followers of the Evil One. These witch-prickers were paid a substantial fee for each witch they found and obviously they were, therefore, determined to convict as many people as they could.

The witch-prickers used long steel needles fitted into wooden or metal handles and using these fearsome instruments they would try to discover some part of a witch's body that proved insensible to pain. This was known as the 'Devil's mark' and if found was considered to be sufficient evidence that the accused person was indeed a follower of Satan. The witch-prickers were cunning enough, however, to know that repeated stabbings of their needle into the same spot would eventually render that spot insensible to pain or feeling. In addition some of the more unscrupulous witch-prickers actually used trick instruments in which the needle could be secretly withdrawn into a hollow handle.

Witch-prickers in Scotland formed themselves into a professional guild and were thus able to demand and to receive extremely high fees for their services.

One of the most famous witch-prickers was a man called John Kincaid who came from Tranent in East Lothian. Kincaid proudly boasted that, by the skilful use of his art, he had sent many notorious witches to the fire and the gallows. Ironically enough, in 1662, the Privy Council ordered Kincaid's arrest and issued a proclamation stating that numerous innocent people had been wrongfully arrested and tortured by people who had no warrant or authority for doing so and who had only acted out of pure greed and malice. This was, however, of little consolation to those poor unfortunate wretches who had already been burned alive as convicted witches. After several weeks in prison Kincaid pleaded to be released on the grounds of his advanced age and the dreadful sufferings he had undergone during his term of imprisonment. After due consideration the Privy Council ordered his release on the strict condition that he 'would prick no more without a legal warrant'.

Another infamous witch-pricker, called Paterson, travelled to

Frontispiece of *The Confessions of Helen Taylor*, from *News from Scotland, 1591* (author's collection)

THE
CONFESSIONS
OF

HELEN TAYLOR IN EYEMOUTH,

AND

MENIE HALYBURTON IN DIRLTON,

ACCUSED OF WITCHCRAFT, 1649.

WITH THE

DECLARATION

OF

JOHN KINCAID, PRICKER.

COPIED FROM THE ORIGINALS.

---

the north of Scotland, making a great deal of money as a result of his witch-finding activities. In one day alone he 'discovered' 18 female witches and one male witch at a place called Wardlaw. Outside Inverness he 'found' a further 18 witches, all of whom were condemned to death. It was then discovered that Paterson was, in fact, a woman disguised as a man and 14 of the 18 condemned witches were immediately released. What happened to the remaining four does not, however, appear to have been recorded.

The Reverend Allan Logan, minister of Torryburn, a small village in the west of Fife, was famed throughout Scotland for his skill in the detection and hunting down of witches. During his Communion services he would suddenly glare fiercely down at his assembled congregation then, pointing his finger, would loudly and dramatically shout: 'You witch-wife, rise from the Tables of the Lord.' So confident was his accusation that on almost every occasion some terrified old woman would instantly hurry from the church to be met outside and arrested by the local bailie and his armed men.

Technically witch-prickers were not recognised in England, despite the fact that they flourished in Scotland and were officially recognised by the Scottish authorities. Professional witch-prickers or witch-finders in fact were often summoned by a town council or a local guild or sometimes even by the anxious minister of a country parish. Scottish witch-prickers might on occasion be asked to examine suspected witches in other localities, however. In Newcastle upon Tyne in 1649 a certain famous Scottish witch-pricker was asked to examine a number of arrested witches. The pricker charged twenty shillings for every witch he found, plus travelling expenses. The local townspeople had been asked to co-operate by giving the names of any they suspected of being witches or involved in the evil crime of witchcraft to the town council. Over 30 unfortunate women were brought to the town hall suspected of being witches. All of them were rudely stripped of their clothing and then the witch-pricker viciously drove long steel pins into different parts of their bodies in order to find the notorious Devil's mark. Most of the women were found guilty and at least 27 of them were set aside for further severe interrogation.

Amongst those present at the initial witch-pricking ceremony was a certain Lieutenant-Colonel Hobson, who seems to have been an unusually shrewd and highly observant person, and who was

John Kincaid, witch-pricker from Tranent (Photo: Charles Grant)

less than happy with the investigation. The Scottish witch-pricker said that he could always tell whether a person suspected of witch-craft was indeed a witch or not, merely by looking at them. Hobson was obviously highly suspicious of him and made little attempt to conceal his intense dislike of both the Scotsman and his evil trade. A well-known and highly respected woman was then brought forward and Hobson said, 'Surely she is not a witch?' to which the witch-finder replied, 'She is and the townspeople have certainly declared so.'

Stripped to the waist and with her clothes pulled high over her head the poor woman had several steel pins thrust deep into her thigh. Her clothes were then dropped down and she was asked whether any foreign bodies had been placed into her body. When she was further examined it was discovered that there was no blood issuing from the wounds inflicted by the witch-pricker's infamous steel pins. The witch-pricker triumphantly declared that the woman was indeed a witch and should therefore suffer the inevitable penalty. Hobson demanded that the woman be brought back and ignoring the furious protestations of the witch-pricker insisted that she be further examined. The witch-pricker, with barely concealed ill grace, then pulled her clothes up to her thighs and once more drove his long steel pins deep into her flesh. Blood instantly gushed forth and the startled witch-pricker very quickly declared, 'She is not a witch, she is completely innocent.'

Eventually this witch-pricker was hanged in his native Scotland, having been charged that 'he was a false pricker and should therefore suffer the penalty'. Unfortunately over 220 innocent women had been put to death as the result of his false accusations – for each of which he had been paid twenty shillings!

8 Torture and execution

In an attempt to stamp out witchcraft in Scotland, the Church, the Law and the various local authorities frequently resorted to savage and cruel methods of intimidation and torture. In fact, Scotland was second only to Germany in the sheer barbarity of its witch trials.

One must remember that once accused of the crime of witchcraft, the 'guilty' person had, in most cases, very little chance of ever escaping the extreme penalty. Once an indictment had been drawn up the accused was not allowed to dispute its accuracy even when it was patently and obviously untrue.

Incredible though it may seem, the accused person was actually forced to pay a fee for each fiendish act of torture committed against him or her. The very cost of the trial and the materials used in the building of the execution fire were deducted from the accused's estate and the balance, if any, forfeited to the Crown.

One of the favourite methods of confirming that someone was a witch was the 'trial by water' and this was, in effect, really a question of 'Hobson's choice' because if the accused floated to the surface he or she was guilty and treated accordingly. Should the unfortunate person sink, however, he or she was considered to be innocent of all charges but was frequently dead by the time the excited spectators and court officials had brought him or her to the surface of the water.

The infamous *Malleus Maleficarum*, the 'Hammer of Witchcraft', first printed in 1486, was the handbook used by all judges, magistrates and those involved in the legal profession who presided at witch trials. This terrible book was the means by which thousands of innocent people – men, women and children – were imprisoned, fiendishly tortured then finally burned (sometimes alive) at the stake. Compiled by Jacobus Sprenger and Heinrich Kramer and published in several different languages, it came out in 13 editions up to 1520 then was further revised in another 16 editions between 1574 and 1669. The *Malleus Maleficarum* literally provided a 'step by step' legal procedure for the interrogation of those suspected of witchcraft, together with the forms of questioning to be used and even the actual answers that would be given.

To extract confessions from those accused of witchcraft, torture

Witch-ducking (printed for Edward Marchant, 1613)

was almost always used. The methods varied slightly from country to country. It should be remembered that in those days imprisonment itself was effectively a form of torture. The gaols were usually stinking, rat-infested dungeons where disease was rife. Starvation, cruel and vicious beatings and – in the case of women – even rape by brutal and insensitive jailors were all too common. The accused were not allowed to make voluntary confessions: confession had to come from the heart, which, it was thought, could only be achieved through torture.

The torture was carefully graded into different stages. The first stage was known as 'preparatory torture' and was intended to force the victim to confess to his or her crimes. This was meant to frighten the accused so that they would prove amenable to intensive questioning. They were first of all stripped of their clothing then taken to the torture chamber, where the executioner would take a fiendish delight in carefully explaining the uses of each of the ghastly instruments to be found there. This included instruments for gouging out the eyes, the dreaded rack, branding irons, spine rollers (for crushing the spine), metal spike-lined chairs which were heated until they were red-hot, and many other terrible devices for inflicting pain.

The victim was often fed on heavily salted food and given drink laced with herring pickle in order to induce a burning thirst. Feet and hands were savagely crushed in iron vices and on many occasions the unfortunate person was stretched on the rack. These methods were actually considered by the interrogators to be 'mild persuasion', not torture as such, and once the victim had confessed, the entry in the court records stated that 'the prisoner confessed without torture'.

The 'final torture' was divided into two separate parts. The first part was known as the 'ordinary torture' and was meant to force the accused to reveal the names of accomplices. The second part was known as the 'extraordinary torture' and consisted of some of the most savage and inhumane methods of inflicting pain ever devised by man. Some of the methods used hardly bear description. Red-hot pincers might be used to tear the victim's flesh, or the feet might be encased in a metal boot then molten lead poured into it. Thumbscrews and even toe screws were viciously applied to the helpless victim.

The 'strappado' and sometimes the terrible torture known as the 'squassation' were also used, especially in Scotland. In the former the victim's arms would be tied behind the back then he or she would be hoisted up by a pulley. Heavy weights were attached to the feet until the shoulders were wrenched from their sockets. There were no visible signs of torture having been applied when this method was used. In the latter form of torture the victims were suddenly dropped from a height to within a few inches of the floor. This resulted in their hands, feet, elbows, limbs and shoulders being dislocated.

It is little wonder that the victims, having been driven almost insane by pain and degradation, were only too ready to confess to all manner of crimes, but if they recanted the forced confession after being brought back to court, they were immediately taken back and savagely tortured again. When one remembers that all of this was apparently carried out in the name of Christianity it becomes almost unbelievable. Yet fortunately there were some humane judges who refused to convict innocent people of so-called witchcraft, although they themselves might then run the risk of being accused of having allowed themselves to become bewitched.

In 1618 occurred a case which demonstrates the depths of stupidity to which the witch-hunters and persecutors had sunk in their frenzied efforts to crush the legions of Satan. Archibald Dein, a burgess of Irvine in Ayrshire, had a young and rather high-spirited wife, Margaret Barclay. Margaret was accused by her in-laws, Janet and John Dein, of a petty theft of which, in fact, she was completely innocent.

When the couple refused to withdraw their unjust accusation Margaret immediately raised an action for slander in the church courts. After hearing both sides of the case the kirk session decided that the entire affair was merely a petty domestic squabble and insisted that Margaret and Janet should shake hands and resume their previous friendship. Both women complied but Margaret afterwards announced to all and sundry that she had agreed only in obedience to the session and that she still retained her ill will against her husband's brother and his wife.

A few days later John Dein, who was captain of a merchant ship, set sail for France. The ship was owned by Andrew Train, Provost of Irvine, who decided to go with the ship in order to supervise some business he hoped to transact in France. As the ship left the harbour Margaret Barclay stood at the quayside and was clearly heard to shout, 'I pray to God that neither sea nor salt water shall bear this ship and I hope that crabs will eat the crew at the bottom of the sea.'

Some time later, when the ship was considerably overdue in returning to Irvine, a vagabond known as John Stewart, who claimed to be able to foretell the future, visited the provost's wife and declared that the ship was lost and that she was now a widow. Corroboration of his story arrived some few days later and it was a foregone conclusion that both Margaret Barclay and John Stewart would be arrested, the former on a charge of sorcery and the latter of being able to foretell the future by supernatural means.

When he was interrogated, John Stewart declared that Margaret Barclay had pleaded with him to teach her magical arts in order that 'she might get gear, kye's milk, love of man, her heart's desire on such persons as had done her wrong and, finally, that she might obtain the fruit of sea and land.' Stewart insisted that he had refused her request because he possessed neither powers of magic nor knowledge or sorcery and was, therefore, unable to help her.

Unfortunately, either as a result of torture or for some peculiar reason of his own, he then proceeded to make a confession implicating Margaret by relating the following tale of supposed witchcraft.

Stewart told the court that shortly after John Dein's ship had set sail he had gone to Margaret Barclay's house and there he had found the accused and two other women busily engaged in making clay figures. One of the clay dolls had a tuft of fair hair inserted in the scalp and was obviously meant to represent Provost Train, who was fair-headed. According to Stewart the unholy trio then proceeded to fashion a ship out of clay and during these weird procedures the Devil, in the shape of a handsome black lap-dog, appeared.

Shortly afterwards the entire company including the Devil went to an empty house near the quay. Stewart later pointed this house out to the magistrates. From the empty house the women and the black dog went to the seaside and threw the clay ship and dolls into the water, after which the sea raged, roared, and became red like the juice of madder in the dyer's cauldron.

Immediately upon hearing this confession, the court ordered that all female acquaintances of Margaret Barclay be brought before it in order that Stewart could identify her two accomplices. Steward had, apparently, no hesitation in picking out a certain Isobel Insh, or Taylor and although the poor woman strenuously denied ever having seen him before she was promptly arrested and locked up in the church belfry. Isobel Insh's own 8-year-old

A pentacle (The Witchery Restaurant, Edinburgh)

93

daughter, Margaret, was brought before the court and the terrified child admitted that she, too, had been present when the clay figures were being made. In addition, the girl went on to say that another woman and a 14-year-old girl had also been in the house. The child's story became more and more incredible as she continued and she confessed that a black man had assisted with the doll-making and that the black dog had continually flashed fire from its nostrils and mouth.

When John Stewart was re-examined he readily agreed that the young Margaret Taylor had been present and he also agreed with the other details of her astonishing confession. Originally Stewart had denied that he possessed the power to foretell the future but suddenly he admitted having the gift of prophecy and then recounted an astonishing tale of the origin of his strange power.

He explained that on one Hallowe'en, 26 years previously, he had been journeying between Monygoif and Clary, in Galway, where he met the King of the Fairies and his entire court. Stewart stated that the King had touched him on the forehead with a white wand and that he had not only been stricken dumb but had lost the sight of one eye. His afflictions had lasted for three years and then one day while in Dublin he had again met the King of the Fairies on Hallowe'en. Once more he was struck lightly on the forehead and miraculously both his speech and his sight were restored. From then on, said Stewart, he had met the fairy folk every Saturday evening and at each meeting they had given him prior knowledge of future happenings.

Isobel Insh was recalled and according to the records 'was put under severe pressure to tell the truth'. It requires little imagination to understand what the phrase 'severe pressure' means and, needless to say, within a very short time the unfortunate woman confessed to having been present during the making of the clay images. She almost confessed to possessing supernatural powers by promising Bailie Duncan, who was also a seaman, that if she was released 'he would never make a bad voyage but would have success in all his dealings by sea and land'.

It was agreed that if she promised to make a full confession on the following day the questioning would stop. That night the terrified woman attempted to escape by climbing out of one of the windows onto the roof of the church. The feat was all the more remarkable when one considers that, according to the court records, she 'had iron bolts, locks, and fetters on her'. Unfortunately, the poor woman slipped and fell to the ground where she lay badly injured until once more taken back into captivity. Five days later Isobel Insh died, loudly protesting her innocence; her death was attributed by the local inhabitants to poison.

A commission was now granted for the trial of the two remaining accused persons, Stewart, the juggler and Margaret Barclay. It is, I think, worth quoting direct from the official trial records and one can only marvel at the phrase used, 'gentle torture'.

My Lord and Earl of Eglintoune (who dwells within the space of one mile to the said burgh) having come to the said burgh at the earnest request of the said justices, for giving to them of his lordship's countenance, concurrence and assistance, in trying of the foresaid devilish practices, conform to the tenor of the foresaid commission, the said John Stewart, for his better preserving to the day of the assize, was put in a sure lockfast booth, where no manner of person might have access to him till the down-sitting of the Justice Court, and for avoiding of putting violent hands on himself, he was very strictly guarded and fettered by the arms, as use is. And upon that same day of the assize, about half an hour before the downsitting of the Justice Court, Mr David Dickson, minister at Irvine, and Mr George Dunbar, minister of Air, having gone to him to exhort him to call on his God for mercy for his bygone wicked and evil life, and that God would of his infinite mercy loose him out of the bonds of the Devil, whom he had served these many years bygone, he acquiesced in their prayer and godly exhortation, and uttered these words:-

I am so straitly guarded that it lies not in my power to get my hand to take off my bonnet, nor to get bread to my mouth.

And immediately after the departing of the two ministers from him, the juggler being sent for at the desire of my Lord Eglintoune, to be confronted with a woman of the burgh of Air, called Janet Bous, who was apprehended by the magistrates of the burgh of Air for witchcraft, and sent to the burgh of Irvine purposely for that affair, he was found by the burgh officers who went about with him, strangled and hanged by the cruik of the door, with a tait of hemp, or a string made of

L'Abomination des Sorciers – the mysteries of witchcraft, by Jasper Isaac, 1614

hemp, supposed to have been his garter, or string of his bonnet, not above the length of two span long, his knees not being from the ground half a span, and was brought out of the house, his life not being totally expelled.

But notwithstanding of whatsoever means used in the contrary for remeid of his life, he revived not, but so ended his life miserably, by the help of the Devil his master.

And because there was then only in life the said Margaret Barclay, and that the persons summoned to pass upon her assize and upon the assize of the juggler who, by the help of the Devil his master, had put violent hands on himself, were all present within the said burgh; therefore, and for eschewing of the like in the person of the said Margaret, our sovereign Lord's justices in that part particularly above-named, constituted by commission after solemn deliberation and advice of the said noble lord, whose concurrence and advice was chiefly required and taken in this matter, concluded with all possible diligence before the downsitting of the Justice Court to put the said Margaret in torture; in respect the Devil, by God's permission, had made her associates, who were the lights of the cause, to be their own 'burrioes' [slayers].

They used the torture underwritten as being most safe and gentle (as the said noble lord assured the said justices), by putting of her two bare legs in a pair of stocks, and thereafter by onlaying of certain iron gauds [bars)] severally one by one, and then eiking and augmenting the weight by laying on more gauds, and in easing of her by offtaking of the iron gauds one or more on occasion offered, which iron gauds were but little short gauds, and broke not the skin of her legs, etc.

After using of the which kind of 'gentle torture', the said Margaret began, according to the increase of the pain, to cry and crave for God's cause to take off her shins the foresaid irons, and she should declare truly the whole matter. Which being removed, she began at her formal denial; and being of new essayed in torture as of befoir, she then uttered these words; 'Take off, take off, and before God I shall show you the whole form.'

And the said irons being of new, upon her faithful promise, removed, she then desired my Lord of Eglintoune, the said four justices, and the said Mr David Dickson, minister of the burgh, Mr George Dunbar, minister of Ayr, and Mr Mitchell Wallace, minister of Kilmarnock, and Mr John Cunninghame, minister of Dalry, and Hugh Kennedy, provost of Ayr, to come by themselves and to remove all others, and she should declare truly, as she should answer to God the whole matter. Whose desire in that being fulfilled she made her confession in this manner, but [i.e. without] any kind of demand, freely, without interrogation; God's name by earnest prayer being called upon for opening of her lips, and easing of her heart, that she, by rendering of the truth, might glorify and magnify his holy name, and disappoint the enemy of her salvation.

Margaret Barclay had continually maintained her complete innocence of all charges brought against her and, in fact, the only real evidence possessed by the court was that she always carried a length of coloured thread and a sprig of rowan. According to Margaret this was used 'to make my cow give milk when it begin to fail'. After the 'gentle torture', however, she, not surprisingly, readily confessed to all of the charges and also implicated a certain Isobel Crawford. This poor woman when arrested immediately admitted her guilt but laid most of the blame on Margaret Barclay.

As the trial continued Margaret's husband, Archibald Dein, appeared with a lawyer to act on her behalf. Margaret promptly retracted her confession and declared that it had been forced from her under severe torture. The jury, however, unanimously found her guilty and pointed out that the torture was not being applied when she made her confession and, therefore, this could only mean that she had made it freely and under no form of duress. Margaret was given no further chance to defend herself and the sentence of the court was that she should be strangled at the stake and her body burned to ashes. The sentence was duly carried out.

Curiously enough Margaret Barclay repeated her confession before she died although she admitted that she had falsely accused Isobel Crawford. Margaret's retraction of her false accusation against Isobel Crawford was completely ignored by the court and again the usual 'gentle methods' of persuasion were applied to force a confession. Once this had been achieved the court pronounced the inevitable sentence, which was duly carried out. Isobel Crawford retracted her confession and died vehemently protesting her complete innocence.

It may seem incredible to us in these more enlightened days to believe that any court could possibly convict innocent people and sentence them to death on such contradictory and flimsy evidence, but one must remember the superstitious dread engendered in those days by even the faintest rumours of witchcraft.

A particularly cruel and unpleasant method of execution sometimes practised in Scotland was burning the accused person alive in a barrel of blazing tar. During the reign of James VI of Scotland, a harmless old woman living in the parish of Irongray, some 7 miles west of Dumfries, was suspected of being a witch. There does not appear to have been any real reason for the accusation apart from the fact that the unfortunate woman lived alone. Like many old people she had the habit of talking to herself and also of holding a conversation with her cat. It was also noticed that she seemed to be able to predict storms and sunshine and her predictions always came true. Despite this extremely flimsy evidence the villagers frequently urged the Bishop of Galloway to punish the old woman. He was, quite naturally, extremely reluctant to do so, especially in view of the lack of any real evidence. Eventually, however, he was forced to order that the old woman be brought before him and an angry mob forcibly dragged her from the tumble-down dwelling. Terrified of the screaming mob, the bishop sentenced her to be drowned in the river. The bloodthirsty crowd of frenzied villagers had, however, already decided on their own cruel method of execution: to the bishop's horror the suspected witch was thrust, screaming, into a barrel of tar which was then set alight and sent rolling down a hill and into the waters of Cluden.

In the year 1704 a small, sleepy fishing village in Fife became the scene of perhaps one of the most notorious cases in the history of Scottish witchcraft. The savage brutality meted out to the victims was incredible, even for those dark days.

The tragic tale began when Beatrix Laing asked the 16-year-old son of the local blacksmith in Pittenweem to forge her some nails. The boy, Patrick Morton, explained that he was busy on an urgent job but would make the nails as soon as he had finished the work he was engaged upon. Beatrix Laing went away muttering under her breath and the young lad was convinced that she was threatening him with evil.

The following day the boy saw her throwing hot embers into a basin of cold water and was immediately convinced that he was being bewitched. In a few days he had lost his normally healthy appetite and, not surprisingly, eventually became so weak that he fell ill and was confined to bed. As the days passed Patrick became subject to fits, his stomach became swollen and he had great difficulty in breathing. In his weakened and feverish condition he became subject to strange and frightening hallucinations and was firmly convinced that Satan himself kept appearing at the foot of his bed.

The local minister, a certain Reverend Patrick Cowper, regularly visited the sick boy and appears to have played upon his already overworked imagination by recounting lurid tales of witchcraft and spell-casting. Eventually, with, it appears, suitable help from the minister, the young boy accused Beatrix Laing of being a witch and of having cast an evil spell upon him. In addition he also gave the minister several other names of local villagers and declared that they were also in league with the Powers of Darkness.

Eager to play his part in fighting the forces of the Devil the minister immediately summoned the members of his presbytery and soon convinced them that Beatrix Laing and her unholy accomplices should all be brought to justice. Although the accused woman was an important person in the village, being the wife of the former village treasurer, she was immediately arrested, as were the other suspects. Before a committee could even be organised to examine them the bailie of Pittenweem placed them in the local gaol and deputised the worst drunkards in the village to guard them.

It appears that although it was common knowledge that the deputised guards were not only drunkards but men of extremely low character, the minister himself ordered them to submit the women to every kind of disgusting degradation possible, including the vilest forms of cruel torture. Beatrix Laing was forced to stay awake for five days and nights and eventually confessed to being a witch. She also named Isobel Adam, Janet Cornfoot and a Mistress Lawson together with several others as being followers of the Devil.

When the unfortunate woman was released from the torturers she immediately retracted her forced confession, and this infuriated the minister who instantly had her beaten then locked in the village stocks. With the hysterical behaviour of the local minister and other members of the council as an example, it is hardly surprising that the rest of the inhabitants of Pittenweem promptly followed suit and subjected the poor woman to further savage indignities. When she was eventually released from the stocks Beatrix Laing was thrown into the thieves' hole, a dungeon in the local gaol which had neither windows nor any form of lighting. She spent the next five months in solitary confinement.

The remainder of the accused were each brutally tortured until they had confessed to their wicked crimes. The so-called trial dragged wearily on for months and during this time one of the accused, Thomas Brown, starved to death in his dungeon.

Some of the more intelligent and enlightened members of the community tried to persuade their fellow commissioners that the accused should be set free and that the only real crime committed

The Black Sabbath, from Oufle's *Imaginations Extravagantes*

had been the stupidity and brutality of the villagers of Pittenweem. Eventually it was agreed that Beatrix Laing and one or two others should be fined the sum of five shillings and set free. Hardly had the prisoners been set free when a mob chased Beatrix Laing from the village and Patrick Cowper, the minister, immediately brought fresh charges against the ones still in custody.

Beatrix Laing managed to reach St Andrews but died in a few months as a result of her ill-treatment while in captivity.

Janet Cornfoot, however, was tortured again and Patrick Cowper himself administered a number of brutal floggings in order to extract a confession. A few days later Janet Cornfoot managed to escape from prison and took refuge with one of the families in the village. When news of her escape became known, the inhabitants of Pittenweem became mad with rage and every house was frantically searched until she was discovered. The terrified woman was dragged to the beach, her hands and feet were tightly bound and a long rope was fastened to her waist. One end of the rope was attached to a ship lying offshore and a crowd of men held the other end. Urged on by the minister she was swung backwards and forwards in the sea until she was almost drowned. Eventually the hysterical mob dragged her onto the sand where blows were rained upon her helpless body by everyone who could get close enough to touch her. A heavy wooden door was placed on top of her and then piles of stones and boulders were heaped upon the door until she was literally pressed to death. Even then the bloodthirsty mob were not satisfied and a horse and sledge were ridden backwards and forwards several times over her body. The local authorities refused to intervene and as a final indignity Patrick Cowper refused to give the dead woman a Christian burial. Incredible though it may be, no action was ever taken to bring any of Janet Cornfoot's murderers to justice, even after Patrick Morton had confessed that his accusations had been totally false.

Fortunately not all of those accused of the crime of witchcraft and sorcery paid the ultimate penalty. Although most of them did, there were a number of curious exceptions.

Bessie Roy, a nurse employed by the family of Lesley of Balquhain, was arrested on a charge of supposed witchcraft. She was accused of having bewitched the milk of a poor woman named Bessie Steel who came seeking alms. Incredibly enough, considering that the year was 1590, the jury found her not guilty and she was set free.

On another occasion not only did an accused witch go free but she successfully turned the tables on her accusers. Katherine Keddie from Prestonpans was taken into custody by Bailie John Rutherford and was very severely assaulted by him and a number of his men. The unfortunate woman was so viciously 'pricked' that she lost a great deal of blood and almost died. She was also forced to remain awake for several nights and in addition was cruelly tortured.

After six weeks of this inhumane treatment the Privy Council ordered her to be set free. Keddie had steadfastly refused even under torture to admit to the charges brought against her and when she was released she immediately brought counter-charges of false imprisonment and defamation against her accusers.

The council decreed that she was completely innocent of all the charges and they severely reprimanded her accusers but because of the 'common error and vulgar practice of others in the like station and capacity' Rutherford and his men went unpunished with the exception of a certain David Cowan, 'pricker', who was sent to the Tolbooth for an indefinite period.

Elizabeth Bathgate, wife of Alexander Rae, maltman of Eyemouth, was arrested in the year 1634 on charges of sorcery. It was alleged that because a certain George Sprot had kept some cloth belonging to the accused, she entered his house and forcibly removed the cloth. It was further alleged that she cursed his young child and gave it an egg containing a foul charm, as a result of which the child died. In addition the accused was also said to have threatened George Sprot and told him that he would never again be able to provide for his wife and family and thereafter George Sprot fell into dire poverty.

The charges also stated that a certain William Donaldson, having called her a witch, became grievously ill and was severely crippled for life. The court was also told that when a Margaret Home borrowed money from the accused's husband in order to buy a horse and a cow both of the animals died mysteriously. The list of her crimes was almost endless – sinking ships, burning barns, mysterious illnesses both of humans and of animals, attendance at Sabbats and meetings with the Devil in lonely places. Incredibly enough Elizabeth Bathgate was actually acquitted of all the charges brought against her and the fortunate woman was set free.

There were several very rare cases when the accused person was actually set free on bail and ordered to appear before the court at a later date. On 10 July 1629 at Leith a certain Alesoun Dempstar who had been 'warded as a witch on the accusation of Marion Mitchell', now abiding trial for witchcraft was released on 300 merks bail (a merk was a Scottish silver coin with a value equivalent to 65p). She was cautioned to appear for trial when so charged. On 8 November in the year 1628 a complaint was received from a certain Margaret Jo of Musselburgh. The accused person complained that she had been kept 12 weeks in prison, fettered and bound in irons, and threatened with trial without a moment's notice by the bailies of the said town. The Lords of Council immediately ordained her to be freed from the irons, and further decided that her trial take place on the 25th instant.

Witch's altar with Book of Shadows (author's collection)

In Edinburgh in 1643 occurred a most unusual case of 'witch-craft'; unusual because the woman, Marion Fisher of Weardrie, was not actually accused of witchcraft as such, but of 'being given up to be ane ordinarie charmer' and she was ordered by the kirk session to undergo the following sentence for her crime: 'To sit in sack-cloth, in the middle of the church, before the congregation... and... it is inacted that if ever schoe be fund to wse [use] any such lyk [like] in tym cumming [time coming] to suffer death as ane reail witche'!

In the year 1597 one man and 23 women were burned for the crime of witchcraft in Aberdeen. James Low, a stabler, had refused to lend an old woman, Janet Wishart, his kiln and barn whereupon Janet promptly, according to the records, cast the evil eye upon the unfortunate man. Low immediately fell sick of a strange wasting disease and as a result of his illness slowly died, as did his wife and only son.

Janet Wishart was also charged that she had caused 12 hens to drop dead at her feet and that she had brought misfortune and ruin upon another innocent family by casting a spell upon them using nine grains of wheat and a twig of rowan.

On one occasion while she was winnowing wheat she had raised a good winnowing wind although the weather was calm. Because of her enchantment she had carried on with her task although the rest of her neighbours were unable to continue because of a lack of suitable wind. Interestingly enough the charm she seems to have used was to place a piece of burning coal at two doors in her house. In addition she made cows give poison instead of milk and bewitched oxen so that they would work for no one else but herself. Janet was also believed to have dismembered bodies hanging on the gallows at Aberdeen Links in order to use certain parts of them as charms.

Janet's son, Thomas Leys, was also charged with practising witchcraft and it was said that he and a group of notorious witches had been seen dancing widdershin around the Market Cross led by none other than the Devil himself.

According to the Dean of Guild's records the costs paid by the town for executing the accused were as follows:

> Thomas Leys £2.13s.4d. for 'peattis, tar-barrelis, fir and coal-lis to burn the said Thomas'.
> Jon Justice also received his due fee for executing him.
> Janet Wishart, mother of Leys, and Isobel Cockie cost £11.10s. for their combined cremation, with an extra ten shillings added for dragging another witch through the town in a cart. (This other witch saved the town additional expense because she hanged herself whilst in prison.)

The costs of witch trials in Scotland, as in Germany and France, were always paid either by the witch or by his or her relatives. If, however, the victim was poor, then either his or her master or the inhabitants of the town or village concerned paid the various expenses incurred so it is hardly surprising, therefore, that the more wealthy the accused the more popular the trial.

The following gives some idea of the disbursement of money when someone was accused of the crime of witchcraft:

> *Execution of two Aberdeen witches, i.e. Janet Wishart and Isobel Crocker in February 1596*
>
> | | |
> |---|---:|
> | 20 loads of peat to burn them | 40s. 0d. |
> | 6 bushels of coal | 24s. 0d. |
> | 4 barrels of tar | 26s. 8d. |
> | Fir and iron barrels | 16s. 8d. |
> | Stake | 16s. 0d. |
> | 24 ft of hangman's rope | 4s. 0d. |

| Carrying peat, coals and barrels up hill | 8s. 4d. |
| Fee for justice | 13s. 4d. |

In 1636 in the month of November, William Coke and his wife, Alison Dick, were condemned to death for the crime of witchcraft. This particular execution took place at Kirkcaldy in Fife and it was apparently the normal practice here for witches to be placed, dressed in rough coats of hemp, inside tarred barrels to facilitate their burning. In this case the costs of the execution were shared by the Kirk and the town council (one must remember that the currency is Scots pounds, which in those days were valued at roughly one-sixth of an English pound):

10 loads of coal	3 Pounds 6s. 8d.
Tar barrel	14s. 0d.
Hangman's rope	6s. 0d.
Hemp coats	3 Pounds 10s. 0d.
Making above	8s. 0d.
Expensed incurred in bringing judge	6s. 0d.
Executioner – for his pains	8 Pounds 14s. 0d.
Executioner's expenses	16s. 4d.

In another case where the witch concerned lived as a tenant on a large estate, her goods were confiscated and sold then applied to the costs of her trial. The balance unpaid was charged to the owner of the estate who owned the cottage where she lived and, in due course, this sum was eventually paid:

Watching of the accused by William Currie and Andrew Gray – time taken 30 days	45 Pounds 0s.
John Kincaid – pricking fee	6 Pounds 0s.
Food and drink for pricker and assistant	4 Pounds 0s.
Gallow stakes	40s.
Making of above	3 Pounds 0s.
Fetching of Haddington hangman	4 Pounds 14s.
Meat, drink and entertainment for above	3 Pounds 0s.
Travelling expenses for above	40s.
Meat and drink for accused	6 Pounds 0s.
Expenses of two officers	10 Pounds 0s.

Between the years 1628 and 1629 there appear in the burgh accounts for Peebles fascinating but somewhat cruel records of the trial of three unfortunate local women accused of witchcraft, who were strangled then burned at the stake on a part of Venlaw called the Calf Knowe. All the terrible details are minutely recorded in the records, with every item of expenditure carefully set down:

Gibbet	4 Pounds 0s.
Fee to William Dikisoun, the schoolmaster, clerk to the process	6 Pounds 0s.
Bread and drink for the 'assytheres' (jurors)	30s. 0d.
'Lockman' (executioner) engaged by the treasurer – charge of two days' wages	3 Pounds 0s.
plus ale ('drucking at his feaing')	26s. 8d.
5 loads of peat, plus a quart of ale for the 'peitman' – total	32s. 6d.
3 loads of coals	36s. 0d.
'Ane turs of hedder'	9s. 0d.
The 'ministrie' were summoned to attend - · Alexander Dikisoun got a pair of shoes for that purpose	20s. 0d.
Tar barrel carried to the spot	3s. 4d.
Hangman's wages	10 Pounds 0s.
Payment to the 'dempster' ('doomster', i.e. one who pronounces judgement), the hangman's son	12s. 0d.
'Thrie faldome [fathoms] small towis' used to bind the witches' hands	30d.
'Four faldome gritt towis' required to 'knitt them up withall'	6s. 8d.

These poor women had apparently been found guilty by the confession of a certain Isobell Graham.

One must also remember that witch-hunting, and the subsequent trial and execution of the accused, provided a prosperous livelihood for many people. Clergymen, doctors, scribes, judges, torturers, guards and even local carpenters all benefited from the proceedings. Even innkeepers made a brisk trade by providing food and drink for the enormous crowds who gathered to watch and gloat over the accused's execution.

Little wonder that witch-hunting remained such a popular pastime and it is understandable that those few who had intelligence enough to oppose it were held in extreme disfavour by the majority of people.

Although witches, and those convicted of sorcery, were usually executed by being strangled then burned at the stake there were several other methods of execution, legal or otherwise! Earlier in this chapter and throughout the book examples of these have been mentioned – witches who were boiled alive, witches who were burned alive in a barrel of blazing tar and the unfortunate few who were burned alive at the stake. Burning alive at the stake without the so-called 'mercy' of being strangled first was normally only used in cases of extreme wickedness. Another penalty was exacted for Robert Erskine and his sisters, Annas and Isobell, who in 1614 were found guilty of consulting with witches, poisoning several innocent people and treasonable murder, and were beheaded at the Market Cross in Edinburgh.

It appears that the earliest recorded witch-burning in Scotland took place in the tenth century when three witches accused of conspiring to murder King Duffus by means of enchantment were put to death at Forres in Morayshire (see 'Introduction').

The last official witch-burning occurred in 1727 in Dornoch when a mother and daughter were brought before Captain David Ross, sheriff-depute of the county. The mother was accused of having used her daughter as 'horse and hattock' – which meant that the girl had been shod by the Devil himself and as a result was lame in both feet and paralysed in the hands. The sheriff-depute found the charges proven and the mother, Janet Horne by name, was condemned to be burned in a tar-barrel. The day chosen for the execution was particularly cold and according to official records, 'And after being brought out to execution, the weather being so severe, Janet Horne sat composedly by the fire prepared to consume her whilst other instruments of death were being got ready.' Janet Horne's daughter was released and eventually married; her child curiously enough was born lame.

In Scotland, witchcraft was a criminal offence from 1563, when it was included in law, until 1736 when it was repealed. After 1736, it was only possible to prosecute for pretended witchcraft, and to impose a maximum penalty of a year's imprisonment!

Nowadays, thanks to a more enlightened and educated age, those who practise the 'Age-Old Religion' or the 'Craft' are able to do so without fear of persecution or imprisonment – or death! And yet, are we really more enlightened, more educated? One still hears of modern-day witches practising white magic who are

A portable altar (shown closed) (author's collection)

hounded by religious fanatics, whose children are tormented at school, of ministers who refuse to accord them the benefit of normal Christian rites. There are still fanatical bigots who thunder against divination, healing and other harmless forms of white magic, who still declaim loudly that 'these are the works of the Devil!' The age-old cry 'burn the witch' can still be heard in the twentieth century, and those who are, in any way, different from the rest of the human race may still go 'in peril of their life'! There are many different roads to the 'kingdom of Heaven' and many different ways of travel – and over the centuries the 'wise woman' has proved time and time again that her way is but one of many. To each, his or her own!

Bibliography

Ansdell, Ian *Strange Tales of Old Edinburgh* (Lang Syne).

Bessy, Maurice *A Pictorial History of Magic and the Supernatural* (Spring Books).

Cameron, Charles W. *Curiosities of Old Edinburgh* (Albyn Press).

Cameron, Isabel *A Highland Chapbook* (Eneas Mackay).

Chambers, Robert *Domestic Annals of Scotland* (W. & R. Chambers).

Drummond, Charles *Tales, Traditions and Antiquities of Leith.*

Encyclopedia of Witchcraft and Demonology (Cathay Books).

Gardner, Gerald *Witchcraft Today* (Arrow).

Ghosts, Witches and Worthies of the Royal Mile Collected (Ken Laird).

Glass, Justine *Witchcraft – the Sixth Sense and us* (Neville Spearman).

Grant, James *Old and New Edinburgh* (Cassell, Petter, Galpin & Co.).

Grillot de Givry, Emile *Picture Museum of Sorcery, Magic and Alchemy* (University Books).

Grimshaw, Kevin *Witchcraft in Great Britain* (unpublished thesis).

Guthrie, E. J. *Strange Old Scots Customs and Superstitions* (Lang Syne).

Haining, Peter *Anatomy of Witchcraft* (Souvenir Press).

Hartland, E. S. *The Science of Fairy Tales* (Walter Scott).

Holzer, Hans *The Truth about Witchcraft* (Arrow).

Hope Robbins, Rossell *The Encyclopedia of Witchcraft and Demonology* (Peter Nevill).

Huson, Paul *Mastering Witchcraft* (Hart-Davis).

Hutin, Serge *Casting Spells.*

Kingston, Jeremy *Witches and Witchcraft* (Aldus Books).

Kirkpatrick Sharpe, C. *The History of Witchcraft in Scotland* (Hamilton, Adams & Co.).

MacGregor, Alasdair Alpin *Strange Tales of the Highlands and Islands* (Lang Syne).

Mackay, John *History of the Barony of Broughton* (John Menzies & Co.).

Macleod, Nicholas A. *Scottish Witchcraft* (James Pike Ltd).

Maple, Eric *The Dark World of Witches* (Robert Hale).

Maple, Eric *Witchcraft* (Octopus Books).

Maxwell Wood, J. *Witchcraft in South-West Scotland* (E. P. Publishing Ltd).

Menen, Aubrey *The Prevalence of Witches* . . . (Penguin).

Michelet, Jules *Satanism and Witchcraft* (Tandem).

Murray, Margaret A. *The God of the Witches* (London).

Murray, Margaret A. *The Witch Cult in Western Europe* (Oxford).

Robertson, D. M. *Longniddry* (Church Publication).

Rohmer, Sax *The Romance of Sorcery* (Methuen).

Scot, Reginald *The Discoverie of Witchcraft* (Dover Publications).

Scott, Sir Walter *Demonology and Witchcraft* (Routledge).

Seabrook, William *Witchcraft* (Sphere).

Seth, Ronald *In the Name of the Devil* (Jarrold).

Sinclar, George *Satan's Invisible World Discovered* (Thomas George Stevenson).

Smith, Janet M. *Barbara Napier* (The Moray Press).

Sprenger, Jakob and Kramer, Prior Heinrich *Malleus Maleficarum* (Pushkin Press).

Stevenson, R. L. *Edinburgh* (Seeley & Co.).

Summers, Montague *A Popular History of Witchcraft* (Kegan Paul).

Summers, Montague *The Geography of Witchcraft* (Routledge & Kegan Paul).

Summers, Montague *The History of Witchcraft and Demonology* (Routledge & Kegan Paul).

Summers, Montague *Witchcraft and Black Magic* (Rider).

Tales of Edinburgh Castle Collected (Lang Syne).

The Secrets of Princes Street and the New Town (Lang Syne).

Thomas, Jack *Witches . . . stay away from my door* (Wolfe).

Tindall, Gillian *A Handbook on Witches* (Mayflower).

Valiente, Doreen *Witchcraft for Tomorrow* (Robert Hale).

Wallace, C. H. *Witchcraft in the World Today* (Tandem).

Wedeck, H. E. A. *Treasury of Witchcraft* (Vision).

Williams, Jay *The Witches* (MacDonald).

Wilson, Daniel F.R.S.S.A. *Memorials of Edinburgh* (Hugh Paton).

Witchhunting in East Lothian Libraries Division, East Lothian District Council.

Wright, William *News from Scotland.*

Documents and manuscripts (unpublished), author's private collection.

Index